Children's Voices: Talk in the Classroom

Bernice E. Cullinan
Editor

International Reading Association
Newark, Delaware 19714, USA

IRA BOARD OF DIRECTORS

The International Reading Association attempts, through its publications, to provide a forum for a wide spectrum of opinions on reading. This policy permits divergent viewpoints without assuming the endorsement of the Association.

Director of Publications   Joan M. Irwin
Managing Editor   Anne Fullerton
Associate Editor   Romayne McElhaney
Assistant Editor   Amy Trefsger
Editorial Assistant   Janet Parrack
Production Department Manager   Iona Sauscermen
Graphic Design Coordinator   Boni Nash
Design Consultant   Larry Husfelt
Desktop Publishing Supervisor   Wendy Mazur
Desktop Publishing   Anette Schuetz-Ruff
Cheryl Strum
Richard James
Proofing   Florence Pratt

Cover and interior illustrations by Dave Bailey.

Library of Congress Cataloging in Publication Data
Children's voices: talk in the classroom/Bernice E. Cullinan, editor.
     p.   cm.
Includes bibliographical references (p.   ) and indexes.
1. Children—United States—Language. 2. Oral communication—United States.
3. Language arts (Elementary)—United States. 4. Classroom management—United States.   I. Cullinan, Bernice E.
LB1139.L3C456   1993   93-13319
372.6'2—dc20   CIP
ISBN 0-87207-381-5

Contents

Foreword

* *

Much talk surrounds the way parents share books with very young children. In fact, Ninio and Bruner (1973) found that one of the first language patterns or frames children develop can occur in a turn-taking routine during story reading. In their study, a mother shared books with her daughter from the time she was 8 months old until she was 18 months. The parent supported the child's dialogue by adjusting her comments about the book so the child could participate more in the reading. By looking at the pictures, reading the text, and connecting the story to real-life experiences, the parent and child talked their way through to the meaning of the story. In literate families where children hear stories read aloud four and five times a day, children talk about their favorite tales, link authors and illustrators with their work, and reread and discuss stories.

When I was growing up both my mother and father read to me, and an older sister kept us all laughing with her telling of "The Elephant's Child" from Rudyard Kipling's *Just So Stories*. In addition, I was fortunate to be able to discuss the books I read with my twin sister. We argued about which ones were the best. My favorite, which I read over and over again, was *The Secret Garden* by Frances Hodgson Burnett, while my twin sister's favorite was *A Little Princess* by the same author. I could tell my sister my real feelings—*A Little Princess* frightened me. I hated Miss Minchin because she was so cruel to Sara Crewe, whereas I loved the mystery of the secret garden where Mary and Colin were restored to glowing health under the loving care of Dickon. One book frightened me; the other fulfilled me. I could share my real feelings with my twin but not in the written or oral book reports required in school. I never wrote a book report on *The Secret Garden*; it was too special to spoil.

The chapters in this book talk about ways to organize classrooms that will support the sharing of books in the same ways that book-loving families share books. Teachers are shown ways to create environments that will encourage literate talk, not discourage it. As children share their feelings and enjoyment of books in literature discussions or through drama, storytelling, or Readers Theatre, they become "classroom communities of readers" (Huck, Hepler, & Hickman, 1993), children who read a wide variety of books, who enjoy reading, and who will become lifelong readers.

Charlotte S. Huck
The Ohio State University (Emeritus)

References

Huck, C.S., Hepler, S.I., & Hickman, J. (1993). *Children's literature in the elementary school* (5th ed.). Orlando, FL: Harcourt Brace.

Ninio, A., & Bruner, J. (1973). The achievement and antecedents of labeling. *Journal of Child Language, 5*, 1-15.

Children's Books

Burnett, F.H. (1987). *The secret garden.* New York: Grosset & Dunlap. (Original work published 1911)

Burnett, F.H. (1963). *A little princess.* (Ill. by T. Tudor). New York: HarperCollins. (Original work published 1905)

Kipling, R. (1991). *Just so stories.* New York: HarperCollins. (Original work published 1902)

Contributors

Bob Barton
Toronto, Ontario

Bernice E. Cullinan
New York University
New York, New York

Sheila M. Fitzgerald
Michigan State University
East Lansing, Michigan

Charlene Klassen
University of Arizona
Tucson, Arizona

Sam Leaton Sebesta
University of Washington
Seattle, Washington

Kathy G. Short
University of Arizona
Tucson, Arizona

Julie E. Wollman-Bonilla
Rhode Island College
Providence, Rhode Island

Introduction

Bernice E. Cullinan

anguage serves a double function: it is both a mode of communication and a medium for representing the world about which we communicate. Jerome Bruner, who probes relations between cognition and speech in *Actual Minds, Possible Worlds*, describes how words shape thought: "How one *talks* comes eventually to be how one *represents* what one talks about" (1986, p. 131). In other words, the way we say something gradually determines the way we understand it; we seem to convince ourselves as we wrap elusive concepts in words.

But as teachers we may discredit talk. We say, "Talk is cheap. Those who merely talk never think." We may even invoke Shakespeare to devalue talk: "A gentleman, nurse, that loves to hear himself talk, and will speak more in a minute than he will stand to in a month" (from *Romeo and Juliet*, Act II) or "Talkers are no good doers" (from *Richard III*, Act I). Noted researcher Don Graves once said to me, "The words I say out of my mouth just seem to float away and disappear in thin air. Once said, they're gone—never to be seen or heard again. But the words I put on paper live longer; they stay there and can be read again and again."

1

On the whole, we give more credence to written words than to spoken ones. And it is true that written words last longer and travel further than spoken ones (unless the spoken ones are taped). Traditionally, we have valued silent classrooms because we tend to equate silence with thinking and with productive work. But research revolutionizes our beliefs about talk.

Research on talk in classrooms shows that students *need* to talk in order to learn and to become competent language users. In fact, the role of talk in learning is crucial. Douglas Barnes (1976) states, "Talk is a major means by which learners explore the relationship between what they already know and new observations or interpretations which they meet." We explain things to ourselves by talking them through.

Students learn by talking. Students (and all learners) formalize elusive concepts as they shape them in words and express them. Putting concepts into language makes them memorable; labels for concepts give us handles to hold on to. Taking ownership of ideas involves putting them into our own words.

Talking helps clarify thoughts. A colleague and I meet to discuss an article, chapter, or speech we are preparing. We find that talking it through helps us see where we are headed and think more clearly about what we want to say. E.M. Forster recounted hearing an old lady ask, "How can I know what I think till I see what I say?" There is a truthful message behind this amusing question, and that truth applies as much to spoken as to written language. We need to hear ourselves say it to believe it—and, sometimes, just to know what "it" is.

Talk aids comprehension. Students who talk about a topic understand it better than students who do not talk about it. When we finish reading a good book, for example, we want to talk about it. Discussion following reading provides more than the opportunity to live in the spell of a good story for a while longer; it increases our understanding of the story by giving us the opportunity to express and share ideas about it. In this way, talk improves and deepens comprehension.

Students need to talk before they write. Writing process researchers show that prewriting conferences improve student writing. Students who talk with a partner about what they want to say will write more effectively than students who begin writing without a conference.

Talking in front of a group develops students' confidence. The axiom "practice makes perfect" applies to talk. Talking in front of a group helps students become increasingly confident as they express their ideas to an interested audience of peers. The self-fulfilling prophecy that confidence begets confidence prevails: We get good at what we practice doing.

Talk provides a window on students' thinking. When students talk about what they think, we can more effectively develop strategies to help them develop their thinking skills. We can use their words as a scaffold to the next level of thought. Their words guide us as we prepare subsequent learning experiences.

Adults can facilitate children's language development by carrying on conversations with them and by giving them opportunities to express themselves. Gordon Wells (1985) suggests four guidelines for adults:

- Treat what the child has to say as worthy of careful attention.
- Do your best to understand what the child means.
- Take the child's meaning as the basis for what you say next.
- In selecting and delivering your messages, take account of the child's ability to understand—that is, to construct an appropriate interpretation (p. 118).

It is important to note, though, that students are more likely to explore the possibilities of talk in small groups of peers than in discussions led by teachers. Although a teacher may say, "Just ignore me—I'll sit here and not say anything," students are affected by the presence. When peer groups meet alone, students will talk more freely. This is not to say that teachers should not participate in class discussions; they should simply be aware that the quantity and quality of talk may be different than in the discussion students have among themselves.

In his 1965 publication *Spoken English*, Andrew Wilkinson states that talk develops from practice in a variety of situations. He maintains that the teacher's job is to provide this variety through numerous activities that encourage children to use their increasing powers of speech. The authors in this book suggest discussions, literature circles, storytelling, creative drama, Readers Theatre, choral reading, and many other techniques for stimulating talk in the classroom.

In this book, Sheila Fitzgerald provides an overview of how oral language activities link to literature in elementary language arts classrooms. She illustrates the ways that oracy and literacy are interwoven and introduces a broad range of activities to enrich children's language development.

Bob Barton shares some tips that worked for him when he began as a weaver of words. He gives us material to begin with and tells us—and our students—how to spin a good tale for an audience. He understands the storyteller's initial nervousness and the progress toward developing a story that captivates listeners in both content and delivery.

Sam Sebesta explores oral language development through creative drama. He suggests guidelines for direct point of view presentations, role playing, and various forms of creative drama such as dramatic play and story enactments. He illustrates the techniques using children's books that lend themselves particularly well to dramatic interpretation. He concludes with a brief review of the research that supports using creative drama.

The concluding chapters explore the numerous benefits of asking children to talk about books. Julie Wollman-Bonilla gives teachers strategies for helping children make connections between books and their background knowledge as well as across books. Through children's voices we can observe their minds working as they construct meaning and become personally engaged with texts. In the final chapter, Kathy Short and Charlene Klassen show a variety of ways to organize literature circles, a highly flexible type of literature discussion group. They show literature circles in action to reveal many possibilities for learning that exist when we encourage children to talk.

Use the ideas set forth here to help you get started in giving your students a chance to talk. It will make your classroom noisier, but it will ring out with the sounds of learning. It will also give you a chance to practice another of the language arts: listening. You may be surprised at what you hear.

References

Barnes, D. (1976). *Communication to curriculum.* Portsmouth, NH: Boynton Cook.

Bruner, J. (1986). *Actual minds, possible worlds.* Boston, MA: Harvard University Press.

Wells, G. (1985). *The meaning makers.* Portsmouth, NH: Heinemann.

Wilkinson, A. (1965). *Spoken English.* Birmingham, UK: University of Birmingham.

Chapter 1

Enriching Oral Language with Literature

Sheila M. Fitzgerald

Russell, a 14-year-old middle schooler, attended weekly sessions at a university clinic because his reading was far below grade level. Even lower than his reading ability was his attitude about reading: he hated it and saw no purpose for it. Madelyn, his tutor at the clinic, was desperate to help him find the joy in and some enthusiasm for reading. One day she brought in a brief Readers Theatre script of the scene from Wilson Rawls's, *Where the Red Fern Grows* in which Billy Coleman tries to explain to his anxious father why he stayed away from home all night. Russell's attention perked up a bit when he found out that he and Madelyn would take parts and "do" the script. After reading silently, Russell read aloud the part of Billy with expression and enthusiasm while Madelyn played the father and the narrator.

Madelyn was thrilled with Russell's initial, tentative interest in Readers Theatre, so she made sure to include at least one script each time they met. Sometimes they repeated a favorite and changed parts; sometimes they tape-recorded their private performance, listened to it, and then discussed how changes would enhance the meaning. Russell frequently asked to repeat the *Red Fern* script, and it wasn't long before he asked if there was a whole book about Billy and his dogs. Madelyn gave him the book as a gift the following week, and Russell asked to reserve time each week for them to read the book together. Perhaps the most telling comment about the success of this approach occurred during Madelyn's final session with Russell. She asked him what part of their work together he liked most. He quickly said, "When we did those plays." Then he paused, peered at his tutor, and asked, "Was that reading?"

Madelyn understood that for children like Russell—and, indeed, for all children—opportunities to transform written words into the more familiar realm of spoken language are exciting and comforting; they enable young readers to concentrate on the meanings they can make of the text and on their own identifications with the feelings the author is trying to convey. In the past, this relationship between reading and oral language was not well understood. This could be because of traditional views of reading, as Gleason (1989) explains:

> For most of this century reading was considered a primarily perceptual, visually based activity, and theories of instruction and remediation were predicated on this assumption.... During the sixties and seventies, however, researchers within the then new paradigm of psycholinguistics challenged this assumption and replaced it with a whole new view. They stated that the nature of reading was language-based (p. 232).

The power that oral language activities have for helping children become less self-conscious about their talents in reading—particularly their talents in reading orally—is one of their central advantages. Many classroom teachers ease children into oral reading through group activities such as choral reading of songs and poems; in a group the voices blend and individual reading miscues do not cause embarrassment. As children gain confidence and interest, they will choose to read parts of the texts independently or will ask to dramatize specific characters and events. Children of all ages also enjoy using a text as the basis to re-create a story in their own words and actions. Through the interaction of literature and oral language in a variety of forms, children's thoughts and emotions develop, their expressive powers flourish, and they become increasingly respectful and analytic of the literature they encounter.

Choral Reading and Choral Speaking

Although the terms "choral reading" and "choral speaking" often are used interchangeably, the former means reading from a printed text while the latter refers to group performance of a memorized piece of prose or poetry. There are good reasons for including both in the curriculum. Choral reading and speaking offer children considerable reading practice because repeated readings are needed to achieve accuracy and a blending of voices. Both help children interpret texts and demonstrate their understanding in the emotions they convey with their voices. Memorizing pieces for choral speaking also ensures that children will always have a few favorite lines tucked away in their heads.

Singing is a special form of choral work that appeals to very young and older children. Songs are particularly valuable for easing children into oral reading unself-consciously because students are soon captivated by lilting melodies and strong rhythms. Teachers can make the lyrics accessible to the whole class by writing them out on a large chart. Fortunately, much good song literature is available, and teachers can choose from a variety of titles appropriate for the age and interests of their students. The counting song *Roll Over!* in a version illustrated by Merle Peek delights both younger and older singers, as do *Walk Together Children*, Ashley Bryan's collection of black American spirituals, and Tom Glaser's version of the perennial favorite *On Top of Spaghetti*; older students find reading and singing challenges in *Fox Went Out on a Chilly Night*, illustrated by Peter Spier. Repeated reading of song lyrics has potential for developing the smooth flow of children's reading as well as for increasing their knowledge of the connection between oral and written language.

While both prose and poetry are appropriate for speaking and reading in chorus, the patterns of poetry's words and rhythms seem to be most successful in elementary classroom work. Nursery rhymes are a natural choice for starting choral speaking with young children, but teachers soon learn they cannot count on all children bringing to school a rich repertoire of favorite Mother Goose jingles. Teachers need to help children learn the common nursery rhymes they may have missed; there are also many less familiar rhymes that children love to memorize and roll off their tongues— such as this one, reprinted in Arnold Lobel's *Gregory Griggs and Other Nursery Rhymes*:

> Gregory Griggs, Gregory Griggs,
> Had twenty-seven different wigs.
> He wore them up, he wore them down,
> To please the people of the town.
> He wore them east, he wore them west,
> And never could tell which one he liked best.

Younger and older children alike can also enjoy memorizing longer poems and reciting them in unison. Memorizing poems for choral speaking is not difficult when the vocabulary is relatively simple and the rhymes strong, but choral reading of more challenging poems can also be rewarding. Young children can easily read favorite short poems aloud in chorus when they have heard them many times. Nikki Giovanni's unrhymed poem "The Drum" from *Spin a Soft Black Song* is a good choice because it speaks in a child's voice about the search for identity and individuality that all children experience. Older children could try poetry that is more complex in vocabulary, construction, and theme. One possible poem to choose is "Macavity" from T.S. Eliot's *Old Possum's Book of Practical Cats*. Macavity, the mystery cat, is a master criminal, and it takes some sophisticated words and phrases to describe him. Children soon want to know the meanings of "powers of levitation," "larder," "rifled," "stifled," and all the other interesting words in the poem. Later teachers will hear these words in children's conversations and see them in the stories they write.

Reading in unison can lead children to identify lines or stanzas in a poem that would be more effective if read by a solo voice, a pair of voices, or a voice with a certain timbre, or to identify lines, stanzas, or refrains that seem to need certain pacing. One favorite poem for reading in parts is "If I Were in Charge of the World" from Judith Viorst's *If I Were in Charge of the World and Other Worries*. Certain poetry anthologies identify the speaking parts but challenge students' interpretive powers by requiring the voices to speak contrapuntally. One such anthology is Paul Fleischman's *Joyful Noise: Poems for Two Voices*. "Fireflies" from that volume paints the insects as flickering night-time calligraphers and challenges two students (or two groups of students) to create glimmering, glowing night writers through the staccato of their voices.

The children themselves should decide how to perform each poem. When they make the decisions, they will work hard to achieve the desired results and to analyze their effectiveness. Problem-solving, creative thinking, critical listening, and persuasive speaking enter into planning a choral reading performance for classmates, other students, or adults.

Literature Discussions and Book Reports

Literature contributes to children's oral language development by suggesting syntactical structures to follow and words to use, and it also causes students to stretch their oral competencies to explain literature experiences to their peers. Most teachers know that literature reflects life and that it helps students understand their own life experiences and the directions their lives might take in the future. These teachers plan frequent opportunities for students to talk to their peers about books that have touched them. They agree with Korda (1986), who wrote as follows:

> Literature—good, bad, and indifferent—shapes our lives. When we are young, it is the stuff of our dreams, fantasies, and ambitions, not only an escape from the far less interesting real world around us, but also a way of learning about things

that all too often can't be learned at home.... All the lessons of life are there, buried in great books and great drama, and the interesting thing is that we absorb them without a sense of being "taught," without effort, for at the same time we are being entertained (p. 104).

Children need many opportunities to share their book experiences with peers. This can be accomplished in small-group discussions guided by the children themselves (a topic that is the focus of chapters 4 and 5 of this volume). If all the children in the group have read the same book, they might guide their conversation by posing a question, such as one of these:

- In what ways are the events in this book like or different from my experiences in life?
- Which character in the book is most like me or most different from me in personality?
- What was the most interesting or unusual part of the book for me?

If all the children in the group have read different books, their discussion might involve describing the books for one another, offering opinions, or searching for common themes or literary elements. Regardless of the details of their organization, group conversations about books help children analyze the reading they do and articulate the ideas and feelings that books generate. They also encourage children to broaden their literary experiences by reading books their peers are enthusiastic about.

In addition to group sharing, more formal book reports can challenge children's oral language powers. Reports do not need to be written and presented for the sole purpose of proving that the book was read. When students have real enthusiasm for a book and want their peers to enjoy it also, they can come up with exciting oral book report formats: dressing up like one of the main characters and telling about the story from that character's point of view; holding a mock television interview with a partner, one child playing the author and one an interviewer; or describing an interesting scene in the book and then dramatizing it. In contrast to the more informal talk that characterizes small-group discussions of books, oral book reports give students practice with the more formal language and delivery style of a presentation.

Dramatic Voice Presentations

Storytelling and Readers Theatre are two energizing ways to involve students more intimately with the literature they hear and read—storytelling because it teaches children to recall the plots, sequence of events, and most telling aspects of characters; Readers Theatre because the performers must interpret the shades of meaning in the script they use to bring the characters and the story to life for an audience.

Storytelling, discussed in more detail in the next chapter, is one of the oldest art forms. Through storytelling, ancient and even more contemporary societies passed on to the young their histories, religious beliefs, mores, and ideals in tales told by master storytellers, parents, and grandparents. Fortunately, there has been a remarkable resurgence of interest in storytelling in the past quarter century, and many school children now enjoy the special relationship that develops between teachers and students during regular storytelling times. Not all teachers, however, are aware of the importance of helping children themselves become storytellers. Young storytellers soon learn the importance of character and setting descriptions, effective beginnings and endings, and plot development and sequence. Through multiple opportunities to retell favorite stories to peers in small groups, children develop oral narrative abilities, deeper respect for the craft of authors, and insights into story development—skills they can transfer to both their reading and writing.

Children can get a successful start as storytellers through group retellings of long-time favorites such as "The Three Pigs" or "The Three Billy Goats Gruff." One child starts by contributing his or her version of the beginning of the story, and other children add sentences in turn until the story is completely told. At first, the teacher and children should expect "errors" in story sequence and forgotten details. Over time, children learn to accept the corrections and additions of their friends because they know these contributions add to the richness of the story the class is telling. Older children may feel greater interest in retelling simple stories if they know they will perform them for children in a lower grade. After a number of successful group retellings, children will be eager to select their own stories to practice and tell individually to a small group of their peers.

Readers Theatre offers another way into dramatic voice presentations. In Readers Theatre children have a script in their hands; they use the author's language, not their own words. The script may be a scene from a favorite book, as was the script from *Where the Red Fern Grows* that piqued Russell's interest in reading the book; it may be a complete brief story such as Leatie Weiss's *My Teacher Sleeps in School* or a chapter from a favorite read-aloud book such as Mordecai Richler's *Jacob Two-Two Meets the Hooded Fang* or Patricia MacLachlan's *Sarah, Plain and Tall.* Teachers can easily develop their own Readers Theatre scripts for use in their classrooms, scripts that maintain the integrity of the language painstakingly created by the author of a favorite piece of literature. For example, the opening scene in E.B. White's *Charlotte's Web* offers children a brief and moving conversation between a child and a parent when Fern's mother explains to her where her father is going with the ax. By removing the "she saids" and creating a narrator's role for the descriptive passages, teachers can quickly create a script for children to use over and over again. Older children can learn to identify scenes that are strong in dialogue and dramatic appeal and can then create their own scripts. When the final scripts are typed, and perhaps laminated, the class will have Readers Theatre materials to use throughout the school year.

With practice in script reading, children learn to bring to life the full range of meanings and emotions of the characters. As they work with their peers to polish Readers Theatre presentations, they evaluate their interpretations and their pacing, success in responding on cue, diction, projection, and other oral reading skills. When the presentation is ready for an audience, the performers sit on chairs or stools and hold folders containing the scripts. Usually only voices and perhaps facial or upper torso body movements are used to convey the story; there are no props or costumes. Sometimes the children might like to create a new performance by

changing parts and presenting the scene again with different interpretations of the characters.

Dramatizations

The line between dramatic voice presentation and dramatization is hazy. Literature can stimulate children to act out stories
with their bodies as well as their voices. Cottrell (1987) describes
the power of dramatization this way:

> Creative drama is an art for children in which they involve
> their whole selves in experiential learning that requires imagi-
> native thinking and creative expression. Through movement
> and pantomime, improvisation, role-playing and characteriza-
> tion, and more, children explore what it means to be a human
> being. Whether the content of the drama is based in reality or
> pure fantasy, children engaged in drama make discoveries
> about themselves and the world (p. 1).

Pantomime is a favorite way to start with dramatic activities. Teachers can select a favorite book with plenty of action and
ask children to act out the parts as the story is read aloud. With
Esphyr Slobodkina's *Caps for Sale*, for example, one child can pantomime the peddler who falls asleep beneath the tree while the rest
of the class can play the monkeys who steal the stack of hats the
peddler has piled on top of his head. The children will undoubtedly
soon want to add monkey sounds to their interpretation of the story.

Creative drama, discussed in detail in chapter 3, is different
from formal scripted plays. There are no scripts in creative drama,
and these little plays are often spontaneous and without costumes,
props, scenery, or even assigned parts. In classroom creative
drama, literature is the inspiration for language and body movements children use to tell a story. Students enjoy planning and performing a variety of dramatizations based on different genres of literature: wordless picture books such as *One Frog Too Many* by
Mercer and Marianna Mayer give children great latitude in creating
appropriate dialogue; Margot Zemach's charming illustrations for
the Yiddish folktale *It Could Always Be Worse* present children
with myriad ideas for their dramatization of that story; "Ishak's

Winter Evening" or one of the other tales in *Stories from the Arabian Nights* (retold by Naomi Lewis) will challenge upper grade children to interpret mystery and fantasy from another culture; a young thespian might develop a fine monologue using A. Wolf's words (as told to author Jon Scieszka) in *The True Story of the 3 Little Pigs.* Dramatizations like these are an extension of the natural play of preschool children. They need to be an important part of both the oral language curriculum and the literature program in the elementary school because they help children make discoveries about their feelings, their bodies, their ability to use language in powerful ways, their favorite books, and their world.

Oracy and Literacy

The neologism "oracy" was coined by the British educator Andrew Wilkinson (1965) to mean "general ability in the skills of speaking and listening" and to be analogous to the familiar term "literacy." Wilkinson and other English educators have taught us much about the importance of oracy: that the old idea that children should be seen and not heard is inappropriate much of the time, that oracy in school programs "is an objective fraught with hopeful possibilities" (Harvey, 1968, p. 3). Quality literature, with its strong emotional appeal for children, is an excellent source for a wide variety of joyous oral language activities in the elementary classroom: for choral readings, discussions and reports about favorite books, voice presentations, and dramatizations. Through these activities children will develop both oracy and literacy and learn about themselves, their peers, and their worlds.

References
Cottrell, J. (1987). *Creative drama in the classroom, grades 4-6.* Lincolnwood, IL: National Textbook.
Gleason, J.B. (1989). *The development of language.* Columbus, OH: Merrill.
Harvey, B. (1968). *The scope of oracy.* Oxford, UK: Pergamon.
Korda, M. (1986, May). The best training for real life—fiction. *Self,* 104.
Wilkinson, A. (1965). *Spoken English.* Birmingham, UK: University of Birmingham.

Children's Books
Bryan, A. (Ed.). (1974). *Walk together children: Black American spirituals.* New York: Atheneum.

Eliot, T.S. (1982). *Old possum's book of practical cats.* (Ill. by E. Gorey.) Orlando, FL: Harcourt Brace.

Fleischman, P. (1988). *Joyful noise: Poems for two voices.* New York: HarperCollins.

Giovanni, N. (1985). *Spin a soft black song.* Toronto, Ont.: HarperCollins.

Glaser, T. (1982). *On top of spaghetti.* New York: Doubleday.

Lewis, N. (Reteller). (1987). *Stories from the Arabian nights.* New York: Henry Holt.

Lobel, A. (1978). *Gregory Griggs and other nursery rhymes.* New York: Greenwillow.

MacLachlan, P. (1985). *Sarah, plain and tall.* New York: HarperCollins.

Mayer, M., & Mayer, M. (1975). *One frog too many.* New York: Dial.

Peek, M. (1981). *Roll over!* New York: Clarion.

Rawls, W. (1962). *Where the red fern grows.* New York: Doubleday.

Richler, M. (1975). *Jacob Two-Two meets the Hooded Fang.* New York: Knopf.

Scieszka, J. (1989). *The true story of the 3 little pigs.* New York: Viking.

Slobodkina, E. (1947). *Caps for sale.* New York: Scholastic.

Spier, P. (1981). *Fox went out on a chilly night.* New York: Penguin.

Viorst, J. (1981). *If I were in charge of the world and other worries.* New York: Macmillan.

Weiss, L. (1984). *My teacher sleeps in school.* New York: Viking.

White, E.B. (1952). *Charlotte's web.* New York: HarperCollins.

Zemach, M. (1976). *It could always be worse: A Yiddish folk tale.* New York: Farrar, Straus & Giroux.

Chapter 2

Storytelling

Bob Barton

F or years, educators have extolled the benefits of storytelling for communicating difficult concepts in a variety of curricular areas and have highlighted its effectiveness in developing rapport with students and winning over reluctant learners. Recently storytelling has been attracting attention among some teachers, not only as an art form, but as a versatile means of developing talking, listening, reading, writing, and drama abilities in their students. But if storytelling has this much to offer, why is it not used routinely in more classrooms? Some teachers cringe at the thought of telling a story without a book in front of them. "Couldn't I just read aloud to my class? Isn't it the same thing?"

Reading aloud to your class is terribly important; so is storytelling. But the two activities are different. To tell a story, the teller must slow time in order to see the story in his or her mind, relate to the characters and their dilemmas, consider personal feelings and responses to capture the truth of the moment, understand the story's significant turning points and have a sense of how to highlight them, and then put this into action while gauging the responses of the listeners in order to mold the flow of the story as it is constructed in the theater of their minds. It is very much improvisational in nature, like participating in a conversation. There is also a powerful sense of intimacy. Reading a story aloud might be better described as enacting a text in which a third party, the author, demands attention of both reader and listener. In *The Reading Environment*, Chambers (1991) says, "In reading aloud the book literally objectifies the experience. Now the relationship is more like two people sharing something other than themselves. Not listener and teller looking at each other, but reader and listener, side by side, looking together at something else."

There really should be no mystique to storytelling. All of us can do it. Throughout our lives we pluck segments from the ongoing flow of existence and shape them into the episodes that we share with others. The skills we use to do this are the same skills we need when taking on a story that is not our own and telling it. In *Shapers and Polishers*, Rosen (1991) encourages classroom teachers to recognize their own strengths: "I believe that teachers are a very talented lot without being tribally aware of it." She argues that if narrative is a powerful force, a liberating activity, a giver of articulateness and worth to students, why shouldn't it be for teachers? "Few teachers of language actually write...or even consciously talk...creatively in the way they expect their students to do. Thus we neither develop our own language as we could nor surprise ourselves by our own skills in manipulating words to creative ends." Storytelling can put this situation to rights.

Getting Started

There are many ways to ease into storytelling and no one does it in quite the same way as anyone else. Many new storytellers find that a good place to begin is by relating personal family stories to students. Often a book that has been shared with the class can be an effective catalyst for home tales. For example, James Stevenson's *Higher on the Door* chronicles the author's memories of the town where he grew up in the 1930s. Any number of examples from this book could trigger remembrances of your own childhood and growing up. With some judicious selection and a little shaping, it's not too difficult to share your memories. If this sort of working with personal stories has appeal, you might enjoy reading *Keeping Family Stories Alive* by Vera Rosenbluth. Not only does Rosenbluth offer practical techniques for exploring family memories, she also includes instructions for assisting children to gather home stories.

One teacher read *Dr. Xargle's Book of Earthlets* by Jeanne Willis to her class. It's a story about space creatures who are taught about human babies. Afterward she asked her students if they knew what they had been famous for as babies. Few did, so that night the students had to interview parents or guardians to find out a story about themselves to tell in class. The next morning, teacher and class treated themselves to a rich diversity of family remembering. In addition to hearing some entertaining stories from their peers, the students realized that people close to them could be significant resources from whom they could learn.

If you feel a bit self-conscious about telling stories on your own in front of the class, try involving the students. *Joining In: An Anthology of Audience Participation Stories and How to Tell Them*, compiled by Teresa Miller, might be a useful resource for you. In it, 18 storytellers discuss their techniques and strategies for encouraging listeners to join them in the telling of a story. The use of repetitive sequence stories that invite students to join in on refrains or create sounds for specific moments can help build your own and your students' confidence in working spontaneously with the voice. "The Strange Visitor" in Joseph Jacobs's collection *English Fairy Tales* is one example of this kind of story:

> A woman was sitting at her reel one night;
> And still she sat, and still she reeled, and still
>   she wished for company.
>
> In came a pair of broad broad soles, and sat down
>   at the fireside;
> And still she sat, and still she reeled, and still
>   she wished for company.

In came a pair of small small legs, and sat down
  on the broad broad soles;
And still she sat, and still she reeled, and still
  she wished for company....

The repetition of "And still she sat, and still she reeled, and still she wished for company" is the obvious place for listeners to join in. You won't have to issue an invitation—after the third repetition, your audience will be with you. As a variation, use Linda Williams's *The Little Old Lady Who Was Not Afraid of Anything*, an exciting modern relative of "The Strange Visitor." They make a great pair to tell together.

Call and response is another common pattern that encourages joining in. Isabel Wilner's *The Poetry Troupe* includes this example of a call-and-response story (reprinted from Bontemps' earlier publication *Golden Slippers*):

"Did you feed my cow?"
  "Yes ma'am!"
"Will you tell me how?"
  "Yes ma'am!"
"Oh, what did you give her?"
  "Corn an' hay."
"Oh, what did you give her?"
  "Corn an' hay...."

Other genres that can lead to student participation include story songs (such as "Frog Went A-Courtin'"), singing games (such as "Old Roger Is Dead and Laid in His Grave"), and stories containing songs or chants, such as this traditional American one, found in Geoffrey Summerfield's *Junior Voices*:

The Kangaroo

A kangaroo sat on an oak,
  To my inkum-kiddy-kum ki-mo,
Watching a tailor mend his coat,
  To my inkum-kiddy-kum ki-mo.

Refrain: Ki-mi-nee-ro'
Kiddy kum keer-o

Ki-mi-nee-ro-ki-mo,
Ba-ba-ba-ba-billy-illy-inkum,
Inkum-kiddy-kum ki-mo.

Bring me my arrow and my bow,
    To my inkum-kiddy-kum ki-mo,
Till I go shoot that kangaroo,
    To my inkum-kiddy-kum ki-mo.
Refrain

The old man fired, he missed his mark,
    To my inkum-kiddy-kum ki-mo,
He shot the old sow through the heart,
    To my inkum-kiddy-kum ki-mo.
Refrain

Bring me some 'lasses in a spoon,
    To my inkum-kiddy-kum ki-mo,
Till I go heal that old sow's wound,
    To my inkum-kiddy-kum ki-mo.
Refrain

Oh now the old sow's dead and gone,
    To my inkum-kiddy-kum ki-mo,
Her little ones go waddling on,
    To my inkum-kiddy-kum ki-mo.
Refrain

If you enjoy singing, *The Singing Sack* compiled by Helen East might be a good resource. It offers 28 song stories (including a musical version of "The Strange Visitor") that students can join in on.

Finding the Right Material

Regardless of how you begin developing your storytelling style, a good story to tell is the first order of business once you get underway. Among the best stories to tell are folktales from around the world. Through centuries of oral transmission and passage through human memory and imagination, their force and drama have been honed, their language polished, the immediacy of their plots made spellbinding, and the truths at their core made timeless. They are the records of human survival throughout the ages as well as unique glimpses into cultures. Is it any wonder that to this day they are mined by artists in all fields for their themes, plots, characters, structures, and styles of telling?

There are, of course, thousands of folktales from which to choose. Faced with such riches, where do you possibly begin to search? You might try jotting down a few themes that interest you (metamorphosis, ingenuity and enterprise, or weak versus strong, for example) and sifting through story collections such as Joanna Coles's *Best Loved Folktales of the World*, Jane Yolen's *Favorite Folktales from around the World*, Angela Carter's *The Old Wives Fairy Tale Book*, or Atelia Clarkson and Gilbert Cross's *World Folktales*. You could also look for a copy of *The Storyteller's Sourcebook* by Margaret Read MacDonald in your local library, find the themes that you've selected, then peruse the lists of stories that illustrate those themes until you find a title that strikes your fancy. You will encounter many familiar titles, but do look also for stories that produce fresh images and offer new perspectives. Your school librarian, public librarian, and local bookseller can help you with additional ideas. Story tapes are a valuable resource, too. Listening to other storytellers can often assist you in finding the stories you need for your students.

Your search is bound to turn up multiple versions of the same story. Some—such as "The Buffalo Girl" in Jan Knappert's *Kings, Gods, and Spirits from African Mythology* and Paul Goble's telling of the Native American *Buffalo Woman*—are cultural variants; others—such as Susan Cooper's and Jane Yolen's different versions of *Tam Lin*—are retellings of tales from the same cultural source by different writers or illustrators. Old tales are often given a facelift by means of transfer from one geographical setting or time period into another. *Dawn* by Molly Bang, for example, is a traditional Japanese tale relocated to 19th-century New England; "The Small Tooth Dog" in *British Folk Tales: New Versions* by Kevin Crossley-Holland is a 19th-century folktale of the "Beauty and the Beast" variety reset in a contemporary urban environment. Some new stories are actually old ones turned inside out by means of a fresh perspective. Jon Scieszka, for example, tells *The True*

Story of the 3 Little Pigs by entering the mind of the poor, maligned wolf and relating the story from his point of view.

Then there are those stories that author Jane Yolen says in *Favorite Folktales from around the World* "are born directly onto the page, strange children of an oral father and a literary mother" (p. 6). These are tales by known authors that have gained wide popularity over a long period—stories by Hans Christian Andersen, Oscar Wilde, or Isaac Bashevis Singer, to name a few. Jack Zipes's anthology *Spells of Enchantment* offers a comprehensive look at these stories.

If shopping among all these possibilities seems daunting, go directly to the hundreds of modern, illustrated retellings of traditional tales that are revitalized and renewed by some of the world's best illustrators and storytellers. Books such as *Oom Razoom* by Diane Wolkstein, *The Talking Eggs* by Robert D. San Souci, and *Orphan Boy* by Tololwa M. Mollel are among the most beautiful available to us. Because the stories represent some of the best of their kind, they can save you hours of searching through collections.

In narrowing your choice, keep in mind that you must like the story you're going to tell or you're not going to do a good job with it. Look for a simple, direct telling in which the plot unfolds crisply and characters are few. Above all, pay attention to what appeals to you. Is there a character whose situation fascinates you? Is there a feeling that haunts you? If so, chances are this story is for you.

Should you wish to develop your own stories, you can borrow traditional plots, themes, or story patterns. For example, a cumulative or sequential pattern (as is found in, say, "This Is the House That Jack Built") might become a container for your own words. You might take several versions of the same story and rearrange and recombine them to achieve the result you want. Occasionally there are aspects of a story that will need to be brought into line with current tastes. Your inventiveness could prove invaluable here. Interpreting a dialect tale in order to make it more accessible for telling and listening, while still retaining some of the sound and rhythm of the original, is an interesting challenge; you might retell a story from the viewpoint of a story character, as

Jon Scieszka does in *The True Story of the 3 Little Pigs*; or a story could be transposed from ancient times to the present. "Telling out of a story" is another option. This involves working up incidents hinted at in a story but not fully developed. These incidents, when lifted from the original, often have marvelous potential to become new stories of their own. Marc Gellman's *Does God Have a Big Toe?* demonstrates telling out of a story brilliantly.

Telling a Tale

The resources listed in the figure on the next page are all useful texts to consult for information about your story selection, preparation for telling, and delivery. To learn a story, you should work in a manner most suited to you. Some people tape-record the story they've chosen and play it over and over as they travel to and from work. Others block out the story as one would a play, dividing it into acts and scenes. Jotting down a skeleton outline of the plot or sketching a rough storyboard are other strategies. Regardless of the approach you take, the aim is to get the story into your own words as quickly as possible.

The next step is to tell the story to yourself, picturing in your mind everything that is happening. Go back to your source material to check for omissions or for significant details, then try telling it again. It's important to take your time, moving back and forth between the source material and your retelling, trying to "see" the story and building back into it bits of vocabulary or phrasing that give it its unique sound. Don't be afraid to retain difficult words or expressions. Within the context of the story they will not pose a problem for your listeners and, indeed, will add resonance to the tale. Memorizing the opening and closing lines can also help you begin and end smoothly.

When you are ready, find a comfortable position, look directly at your audience, and tell the story in your natural voice, just as if you were having a conversation. Beginning storytellers often worry about making the story interesting and sometimes resort to strategies that wind up getting between the listeners and the story (trying to speak in a dialect they have not mastered, for example). Some storytellers use props such as puppets and flannel boards, overhead projectors and story quilts to good effect, but they

Additional Resources for Storytellers

Barton, Bob. (1986). *Tell Me Another.* Portsmouth, NH: Heinemann.

Bauer, Carolyn Feller. (1979). *The Storyteller's Handbook.* Chicago, IL: American Library Association.

Champlin, Connie, & Refro, Nancy. (1985). *Storytelling with Puppets.* Chicago, IL: American Library Association.

Greene, Ellin, & Shannon, George. (1986). *Storytelling: A Selected Bibliography.* New York: Garland.

Livo, Norma, & Reitz, Sandra A. (1986). *Storytelling: Process and Practice.* Englewood, CO: Libraries Unlimited.

Pellowski, Anne. (1984). *The Story Vine: A Source Book of Unusual and Easy-to-Tell Stories from around the World.* New York: Macmillan.

Pellowski, Anne. (1990). *Hidden Stories in Plants.* New York: Macmillan.

are not essential. If you've chosen well, you need only concentrate on the tale and permit it to do its work. You won't be disappointed.

At the conclusion there's no need to ask questions or teach a lesson. Allow the story to settle into the landscape of your listeners' imaginations. They'll let you know if there's anything they want to discuss. They'll also let you know if they have stories of their own to tell.

There is a wonderful story by Antonia Barber entitled *The Enchanter's Daughter*, in which a young woman who has been denied knowledge of her past to the extent that she has not been given a name, discovers in storybooks that there are worlds far different from the one she inhabits. She determines to escape her powerful father, the enchanter, in order to find her own story on the other side of the treacherous white mountains that surround her home. Whenever questions about children telling stories arise, this tale comes to my mind, for it is in recalling past events that our students come to terms with their own identities and, in the process, gain a sense of significance and self-respect. In *Black Sheep and Kissing Cousins*, Stone (1988) discusses this at length:

> All of us, long after we've left our original families, keep at least some of those stories with us, and they continue to matter but sometimes in new ways. At moments of major life transitions, we may claim certain of our stories, take them over, make them part of us instead of making ourselves part of them. We are always in conversation with them one way or another (p. 8).

Encouraging students to use their own backgrounds as a vehicle for talk and sharing is a natural way to engage them in storytelling. Through this experience they collect their personal stories and develop the skills of asking questions and verbalizing about self and family. In addition, they are provided with the opportunity to display pride in their backgrounds and to discover that some feelings, values, and ideas are universal and timeless. Your role is extremely important here, for by helping students to understand the significance of their personal stories you will also help them accept and appreciate the contributions of fellow students in a positive, open manner. Time for our students to reflect on their own and their peers' lives and to better understand their hopes, fears, conflicts, and predicaments can have a powerful impact on classroom learning and, indeed, on the community.

There are ever so many starting points: stories of how students got their names, family journeys, favorite family possessions and the stories behind them, grandparent stories, family pet stories, and stories explaining day-to-day phenomena students might be curious about (where *does* thunder come from?). Each family has its own special language and traditions, and these can yield stories centered around family sayings and proverbs, riddles, jokes, and puns. "A heap sees, but few knows," a familiar saying in North Carolina, or "There's only one thing worse than a back-seat driver and that's a cook in a rocking chair," something that might be heard in New Brunswick, might be the inspiration for family stories for students from those areas.

The recent reissue of *I Saw Esau*, Iona and Peter Opie's collection of generations-old rhymes and chants from children's games and pastimes, serves as a reminder of the existence of an oral tradition in the lives of our students. From the words of clapping games, jump-rope rhymes, and string games to choosing who's "It" for a game of tag, there is a wealth of material to be collected, compared, extended, sung, chanted, and played out. There is no livelier example of children's creativity with language than the intricate tongue twisters, nonsense rhymes, and game chants of street and playground. This material also serves as an important bridge to other traditional material, such as nursery rhymes, simple narrative poetry, and ballads such as "The Rich Old Lady" (shown below), found in Richard Chase's *American Folk Tales and Songs*. It's all grist for the story mill that can be used to help students find their voices when telling the stories of others.

The Rich Old Lady

A rich old lady in our town,
In our town did dwell;
She loved her husband dearly,
But another man twice as well.
 Sing Too de um! Sing Too de um!
 Whack! Fa lal a day!

She was listenin' in at the door one day,
When she heard the old man say
If you sniffed a few old marrow bones
It would take your sight away.
 Sing Too de um!...

So she went down to the butcher's shop
To see what she could find;
She wanted to buy a thing or two
To make her old man blind.
 Sing Too de um!...

She bought twelve dozen old marrow bones,
She made him sniff them all;
Says he, "Old lady, I now am blind,
I cannot see at all."

Sing Too de um!...

"And I would like to drown myself
If I could only see—"
"Just take my hand, dear husband,
And come along with me."
Sing Too de um!...

She bundled him up in his old gray coat,
She led him to the brim.
Says he, "I cannot drown myself
Unless—you push me in."
Sing Too de um!...

The old lady went up on the bank
To make a running dash;
The old man stepped a little to the side—
And in she went with a splash.
Sing Too de um!...

She bubbled and gurgled and bawled out
As loud as she could squall.
Says he, "Old lady, I'm so blind
I can't see you at all."
Sing Too de um!...

The old man being kind-hearted
And knowing she could not swim,
He went and cut him a very long pole
And—pushed her further in.
Sing Too de um!...

Our students must work with the mythic stories too, the stories that explore powerful emotions such as love, hate, fear, joy, and the struggle between good and evil. Don't rush students into performance of these stories.

Making Connections

Classroom storytelling is multifaceted and there are many aspects of it that deserve our attention. Besides the actual story-telling performance, these aspects include overlapping elements of listening, responding, retelling, and extending, which when combined give some indication of the potential of storytelling in th classroom.

Listening. As mentioned at the beginning of this chapter, I believe that the story listener creates the story in the "theater of the mind," in company with the storyteller. As they listen, students make pictures in their minds, revise the pictures as they absorb new information, attempt to figure out the story's direction, become emotionally involved with characters, and constantly judge whether the story is worth all the effort and attention they are putting into it.

Talking with our students about their listening experience after the story has been told is an important part in the development of their story sense. Because listeners' experiences are unique, telling the story of their listening affords students the opportunity to reflect on the story each of them has made from the story they've heard; it also suggests to them new ways to listen. If illustrated versions of the story are available, they can be used as another source to help students compare and contrast what they have imagined with the imaginings of an experienced illustrator. And this talk of listening will lead directly into talk of personal responses.

Responding. One teacher commented this way about the Alfred Noyes poem "When Daddy Fell into the Pond":

> Every time I hear that poem, I see my father, fully clothed, standing at the edge of our boat dock proudly pointing out to my mother the repair job he had just done on the guard rail. Moments later he gives it a good tug and the whole thing breaks away and there's my father thrashing about in the water, fuming, with one of his shoes drifting placidly out to the center of the lake.

As this teacher demonstrates, listeners—our students included— bring their own life experiences to bear on the stories they hear. The interpretation of the story delivered by the teller also influences how listeners' feelings will be directed. Time to explore thoughts and feelings about story characters and events

…orative discussion is an important part of the story

…ple drama techniques—such as interviewing story
…point-of-view retelling, or improvising key moments
from … story—can be used effectively to help students develop
their thinking and feeling about story characters. Initial responses
often change sharply as students begin to appreciate the complexities of story characters or the dilemmas they have faced in struggling to make decisions. Time to get inside a story situation and
fully appreciate a character's point of view can go a long way
toward helping students make a story their own. And this responding will lead to retelling.

Retelling. Story retelling offers students opportunities to
make exciting discoveries. Performing the story in a polished way
is not the primary aim; shaping it, restructuring it, and finding out
what in the story matters to them is. When a story is told and then
shared in small storytelling groups in which the story is retold by
being passed from member to member in brief turns, many possibilities arise. The story may re-emerge from the viewpoint of specific story characters, invented characters, or inanimate objects.
These "eye witness" retellings often support students' attempts to
find out more about the motives behind the actions of story characters. Parts of the story that might have appeared insignificant at
first suddenly take on new meaning as they are elaborated on in the
retelling. New bits (chants, sayings, additional dialogue) get added
and new endings—still completely within the spirit and intent of
the story—are often incorporated. These retellings also offer an
opportunity for students to come to an understanding about "tun-
ing" a story. How would it sound if it were told as a ghost story? A
tall tale? A memoir? A cautionary tale?

The more students come to know the story, the greater confidence they display in their work in responding to and retelling it.
At the same time, the story grows in memory and imagination. As
the students rework and reshape the material, they become part of
the long history of change, adaptation, and reinterpretation that has
characterized storytelling since the dawn of humanity.

Extending. When students have spent time listening to one
another's thinking about a story, have dug deeply into the fabric of

the story, examining its problems, meeting its characters, and probing its nooks and crannies, and have played an active role in restructuring it, they may wish to capture their new ideas in the form of another story, a painting, a sculpture or model, drama, photography, dance, and so on. If the students choose to share these reinterpretations of whatever form with their peers, they have come full circle: the story and the storytelling live again, less as clones of the original than as the product of keen insights, fresh images, and new energy.

References

Chambers, A. (1991). *The reading environment*. Stroud, Glos., UK: Thimble Press.

MacDonald, M.R. (1982). *The storyteller's sourcebook*. New York: Neal-Schuman.

Miller, T. (1988). *Joining in: An anthology of audience participation stories and how to tell them*. Cambridge, MA: Yellow Moon Press.

Rosen, B. (1991). *Shapers and polishers*. London: Mary Glasgow.

Rosenbluth, V. (1990). *Keeping family stories alive*. Vancouver, B.C.: Hartley & Marks.

Stone, E. (1988). *Black sheep and kissing cousins*. New York: Times.

Children's Books

Bang, M. (1983). *Dawn*. New York: Morrow.

Barber, A. (1987). *The enchanter's daughter*. London: Cape.

Bontemps, A. (1941). *Golden slippers*. New York: HarperCollins.

Carter, A. (1990). *The old wives fairy tale book*. New York: Pantheon.

Chase, R. (1956). *American folk tales and songs*. New York: Signet.

Clarkson, A., & Cross, G.B. (1980). *World folktales: A Scribner resource collection*. New York: Scribner's.

Cole, J. (1982). *Best loved folktales of the world*. New York: Anchor/Doubleday.

Cooper, S. (1991). *Tam Lin*. New York: McElderry.

Crossley-Holland, K. (1987). *British folk tales: New versions*. New York: Orchard.

East, H. (1989). *The singing sack*. London: A&C Black.

Gellman, M. (1989). *Does God have a big toe? Stories about stories in the Bible*. New York: HarperCollins.

Goble, P. (1984). *Buffalo woman*. New York: Bradbury.

Jacobs, J. (1967). *English fairy tales*. New York: Dover.

Knappert, J. (1986). *Kings, gods, and spirits from African mythology*. New York: Schocken.

Mollel, T.M. (1990). *Orphan boy*. Boston, MA: Clarion.

Opie, I., & Opie, P. (1992). *I saw Esau*. Cambridge, MA: Candlewick.

San Souci, R.D. (1989). *The talking eggs*. New York: Dial.

Scieszka, J. (1989). *The true story of the 3 little pigs*. New York: Viking.

Stevenson, J. (1987). *Higher on the door*. New York: Greenwillow.

Summerfield, G. (1970). *Junior voices*. Harmondsworth, Middlesex, UK: Penguin.

Williams, L. (1986). *The little old lady who was not afraid of anything*. New York: Crowell.

Willis, J. (1988). *Dr. Xargle's book of earthlets*. London: Andersen. (Published in the U.S. by Dutton as *Earthlets as explained by Professor Xargle*.)

Wilner, I. (1977). *The poetry troupe: Poems to read aloud*. New York: Scribner's.

Wolkstein, D. (1991). *Oom razoom, or go I know not where, bring back I know not what*. New York: Morrow.

Yolen, J. (1986). *Favorite folktales from around the world*. New York: Pantheon.

Yolen, J. (1991). *Tam Lin*. Boston, MA: Houghton Mifflin.

Zipes, J. (1991). *Spells of enchantment: The wondrous fairy tales of Western culture*. New York: Viking.

Chapter 3

Creative Drama and Language Arts

Sam Leaton Sebesta

A h! The memories of my aunt, who became a drama teacher but remembers most clearly the drama of her childhood in a litte Kansas town in the 1920s:

At certain times during the school year, mainly holidays and spring, the teacher passed out play scripts and assigned parts, which we dutifully underlined and memorized. Rehearsals were for "blocking action," a term I thought was borrowed from football. Mothers sewed costumes; fathers and the principal went to school one Saturday and painted scenery on flats covered in stretched muslin.

By the time the play got put on, we all knew each other's lines, though we sometimes forgot our own. Some of us spoke VERY LOUDLY, as we'd been told to do. Others couldn't find their voice boxes anywhere when they were on the stage. It didn't matter. Everyone applauded at the end, even the babies. On the way home each parent assured each child that he or she had been the best one in the school play.

As you can see, drama in the form of traditional play production served a community purpose then; I think it still may do so. I would not dismiss it—not for the world—but there is more to drama than putting on a scripted play. I think it is this other realm of drama that we need to enter as we teach literature and the language arts. "Creative drama," the preferred term for the realm I mean, does not begin with a script; sometimes it doesn't even begin with a story. It is improvisational, which means that you set a purpose and then make up your drama as you go along. In that way, creative drama mirrors life, which takes planning but has no script.

I grant that it sounds a bit disconcerting—especially when a current teaching model is direct instruction with predetermined, required outcomes—but it really isn't a free-for-all. A creative drama session should not be 30 minutes of bedlam. In this chapter, I suggest ways it can take place within the classroom and without the trauma.

Beginnings

Pushing back the desks or going to the gym to slide around in socks may not be the best way to begin drama. Making small but significant changes in what is ordinarily done in reading and writing sessions may be a better way to start.

Direct POV. Everyone with school experience is familiar with the "feel" question. It goes like this: "How do you think Mrs. Pig felt when she sent her three little pig children into the wide, wide world?" or "How did Mary Lennox feel when she opened the door to the secret garden that first time?" Try answering those questions yourself. You are likely to drag out some tired, abstract adjectives: sad, worried, strange, surprised, bewildered. No matter how well you do at describing the feelings, you are still standing outside the story looking in.

Drama begins with becoming the character you are reading, telling, or writing about. To cut through the abstract and enter the action, change "feel" questions to direct point of view, or POV: "Be Mrs. Pig. Show what you said and did..." and "Be Mary Lennox from *The Secret Garden*. Open the door. What did you say years afterward about that moment?"

Almost any situation in a story, narrative poem, biography, or social studies text can begin to come to life through the direct POV technique. Tell students to *be* the character and respond to questions as if being interviewed, using the first-person "I." Sometimes you can probe—"Tell us more"—and sometimes you can ask for action—"Get up and show us exactly how you opened that door and reacted to what you saw."

Role playing. Prediction and problem solving get considerable attention in reading and language arts classes. In basal readers published in the United States in the early 1990s, for instance, 52 percent of the literature-based questions are devoted to "predict-hypothesize-extrapolate" items (Sebesta & Monson, 1992). Research and practice seem to agree: good readers predict, and then they read on to see if they're right. When good readers become authors, they try to surprise their own readers, upsetting prediction without losing credibility.

Here is where role playing comes in. You've already begun to use direct POV; now extend it. Have two or more students use direct POV and then extend the dialogue and actions to show what might happen next. Here is an example.

In Harry Allard's *The Cactus Flower Bakery*, sad Sunny MacFarland lives alone in the middle of a Texas desert along Route 126. Her generous invitations to passersby to join her for refreshments are all rejected—violently so. Why? Well, Sunny is a rattlesnake. Despite her pleasant nature, everyone is scared to death of her. So what can she do to take charge of her fate the next time someone comes along? Go ahead. Have your students use direct POV to tell what Sunny will do, or to get answers from everyone, give out scraps of paper (the kind that might blow across a Texas desert) and have each student quick-write Sunny's plan. But don't stop there. Decide on two or three promising ideas and pick actors to play Sunny and whoever else comes along. Raise an imaginary curtain or turn on an imaginary video camera. Don't let the enactment ramble. Urge it ahead, stopping as soon as the prediction is clear. Then try another and evaluate. Does the solution make sense? Is it credible? Is it wise? After two or three enactments, readers can return to the story to see how the author and Sunny dealt with the problem.

Role playing, then, enlivens instruction in problem solving and prediction. It is not very far from the problem solving and prediction we do in our lives, when we plan ahead by playing out a scenario in our minds or actually rehearsing what we would say or do if a situation arises.

Sessions

Sooner or later, brief bits inserted into a reading or writing lesson evolve into more involved undertakings of creative drama. Stewig (1983) suggests that these times be called sessions, not lessons. They are for improvising and interpreting, not for adhering to a pattern. But short or long, done in a limited area of a crowded classroom or in a wide-open space, these sessions take planning. They don't start with a general announcement such as "Today let's act out the story"; they start instead with small guided steps.

Preparation. Drama begins with the body; as McCaslin (1990) puts it, "Movement is preferred to a verbal beginning at every age level" (p. 56). Start with movement to music. Move your own way in time to the music, then in double time, then in slow motion. Or start with a "space walk" in which the players inside an invisible bubble float through make-believe space, moving about and greeting one another silently and without touching. Two groups on either side of a line on the moon's surface can volley an invisible ball back and forth, or they can form two lines to play tug of war with an invisible rope (a very difficult task, by the way, that is best prepared for by beginning outdoors with real rope). Pantomime warm-up ideas are endless and of varied complexity (many are given in the sources cited at the end of this chapter). I avoid silly ones such as penguins playing Ping-Pong; I like best the ones that lead naturally to characters that can be played, such as the varied, contrasting animals in Eric Kimmel's retellings of *Anansi and the Moss-Covered Rock* and *Anansi Goes Fishing*.

These start-ups to creative drama take confidence, skill, and ingenuity on the part of students and teacher. Remember, the first aim is improvisation, not imitation. You must let students know that they are to figure out what to do, not to copy your model. Concentration will need to supplant self-consciousness or showing off. Gradually, with practice and encouragement, students will learn to concentrate, to see that invisible ball or rope, to become that character whose movements they are miming. Tell them it's like swimming—you don't do the 50-meter butterfly the first time you get in the pool.

Dramatic play. The preparation I have just described may lead to dramatic play, which focuses on setting and situation without predetermined plot. Use pictures and a social studies text, for instance, to visualize the California Gold Rush of the mid-1800s. Bring in, if possible, some realia—objects for panning gold or making a sluice gate, and a few items of clothing of the period. Each player describes who he or she will be, maybe in words along these lines: "I'm called Lucky. Everybody tries to pan in my claim because I found a gold nugget here last week." At a signal, all players do their part to enact a scene along a stream in Gold Rush times. The scene may be brief. At your signal, it stops. Then players talk about what they need to know to make it more real. Now they have need to read more about the Gold Rush, and thereby will place themselves in that historical period and place.

Dramatic play may be used to build the scene around characters real or fictional. After reading biographies of Harriet Tubman, you can play her return to help slaves escape by the Underground Railroad, using walking sticks and packs, bandages, a lantern, and other realia. In chapter nine of Katherine Paterson's *Lyddie*, the weaving-room setting is crucial to the story because it requires readers to experience life in a textile mill in Massachusetts in the 1840s; the setting moves closer when you follow the novel's description as a guide to dramatic play.

There is really nothing artificial about this form of creative drama. We all engage in dramatic play in our lives, whether we call it that or not. The child with a toy airplane becomes a fighter pilot; tourists headed off to a foreign land visualize what they'll do and what might happen to them. We may even "act it out" physically. Recently I came across a worker at a construction site who was operating a wheelbarrow and uttering an unmistakable "putt-putt-putt" as he moved along. In his dramatic play, he had become a truck driver! One line of thinking discourages dramatic play as part of putting away childish things and, indeed, it may not appear to be a clear route to directed reading, writing, and oracy. But another line of thinking is that dramatic play gives motive to learning. More than that, it applies imagery and involvement that are lacking when verbalization is not rooted in experience. For a full discussion of this technique and its merits, turn to the work of Dorothy Heathcote related in Johnson and O'Neill (1984).

Story Enactments

Stories show us connections among events. Story characters interact with one another, sometimes in conflict and sometimes in common effort. In stories we examine problems or goals and how they are—or are not—solved or attained. Heath (1982) shows how early experiences of stories influence success in school, especially in literacy. The importance of participating in story and connecting story to one's own life cannot be denied.

Drama is one means of providing opportunities for participating. As one teacher remarked after a drama workshop, "When you act out a story, you feel it in your bones." Story enactments can be based on any genre. They may be used to provoke curiosity before reading historical fiction. For example, you can help students play the crucial homecoming scene (chapter 18) in Andrea Wyman's *Red Sky at Morning*: Papa comes home to Indiana all the way from Oregon, but why does joy turn to doubt and suspicion? Or, to help readers "see" exact detail, dramatize any of the scenes of experiment in Russell Freedman's biography *The Wright Brothers: How They Invented the Airplane.*

In these sessions, the teacher becomes a leader who assists in the process but does not dictate it. Spolin (1986) elaborates on the leader's job:

1. Help players *focus.* What is the mood and the main idea of the scene to be played?

2. *Side-coach.* As the scene is played and replayed, the leader suggests and questions in order to aid characterization and focus.

3. *Evaluate.* What went well? What needs to be improved?

Here are some suggestions that might guide the way as you move to more elaborate sessions.

Story theater. Try this technique with folklore or any narrative with heavy action. At its simplest, you tell the story or read it slowly, with long pauses to let the players perform the action in pantomime. At first, you can assign roles and give practice in movement ahead of time; later a story theater session can be more spontaneous, with volunteers stepping forward and assuming the roles of new characters as they are introduced. Experienced players may even step in as the important scenery. Here are a few examples.

Play *Mufaro's Beautiful Daughters: An African Tale* at least twice: once before you show the book and once after students have had the great pleasure of examining John Steptoe's vivid "you are there" paintings. You may notice the influence of these illustrations on your players in the second story theater enactment. I use name tags for the main players: Manyara and Nyasha, sisters alike in looks but opposite in their ways of looking at the world, and the Great King, who wants a wife and (as it turns out) is willing to transform himself into other things in order to test his subjects. Help players elaborate on their enactment: for instance, they will need to add movement and stage business to show the bad temper and selfishness of Manyara and contrast this with the direct manner and kindness of Nyasha. This splendid tale, with its constant invention and movement, plays well in story theater. Eventually let it be told entirely through mime, but add a drum so that, to everyone's surprise, it becomes dance.

Donald Charles's *Chancay and the Secret of Fire*, a rousing adventure based on an ancient Peruvian tapestry, is so intricate and challenging that it may take you two or three story theater sessions to do justice to the hero's journey to find fire. You will have fun with a talking fish, a valley of spiders, a field of snakes, and a mountain pass filled with pumas. I rather suspect that the ancient Peruvians would approve of your story theater.

Close study of the sparse text and elaborate painted drawings of Demi's *The Artist and the Architect* will pay off in a powerful story theater enactment. Here you will need skilled players to portray the all-important scenery: a platform with a removable stone slab leading to a secret tunnel beneath the public square. Everything depends on that setting. Creating it will be a challenge for your most skilled portrayers. Let them work it out, and while they are at it, let them decide what to do about the ending: did the architect carry out his vengeful plan?

Adding dialogue. The direction to have students "write a play and then perform it" may be backward. If you are seeking dialogue or monologue that is vibrantly alive, it's often better to help young people speak it first, refine it, replay it, and then (if you and they wish) write it down. Players who mime action tales for story theater can repeat the performance, this time without a teller or reader—instead they should add spontaneous dialogue as they move. This is a good way to start.

When dialogue is added, a range of more reflective literature becomes accessible. Folklore's fast flow from event to event slows down so that scenes are more fully developed. Rather than attempting to dramatize a whole narrative, you might devote your drama sessions to one or two crucial scenes. In chapter seven of Judy Delton's *Lights, Action, Land-ho!*, for example, all the Pee Wee Scouts have their own moment before the movie camera. Seized with ambition for stardom, they tap dance, play violin, or recite "To be or not to be...." Trouble is, the movie is supposed to be about the arrival of Columbus. There is plenty of action and there are just enough lines to suggest the confusion of cast and crew. It's quite a scene, a hilarious possibility for an early session of creative drama in which players perform the action and elaborate on the dialogue. In chapter six of Lensey Namioka's *Yang the Youngest and His Terrible Ear* there's a wonderful, playable scene in which Yang's best friend hides behind a screen and plays Haydn beautifully on the violin, while Yang himself pretends to play in front of an audience that includes his music-loving parents. The hilarity turns to amazement and revelation. Once again, a drama session can include spontaneous dialogue. Add a string quartet too, if you can.

Performing written dialogue. Whole scenes rich with dialogue appear in good books for young people. Emphasis on talk that furthers plot while portraying characters in cooperation or conflict seems to be growing. The dialogue is exceptional in two books by Avi: *Nothing But the Truth* and *"Who Was That Masked Man, Anyway?"* The first breaks the narrative to present scenes in play script; the second is a 170-page tour de force written entirely in dialogue—without even a "he said"! *WKID: Easy Radio Plays* is a recent book of short scripts; *The Herbie Jones Reader's Theater* is a model of how you can convert modern dialogue into script form.

How do you enliven written dialogue through drama? A temptation is to give players the book or script and direct them to "act out" scenes as they read. It doesn't work, not even for adults. You can't read dialogue well while moving around. Instead, try a creative drama sequence. Start by assigning characters, who extemporize speech and movement until they have the focus. Side-coach and evaluate until there's reality to the playing. *Then* bring out the scripts. At this point, action stops and performers put all the force of the scene into their voices. If that sounds weak, play a tape of old radio shows. There's never any doubt that the Lone Ranger is lurking behind the sagebrush to nab the gunman; Sky King and Penny really do stand on the brink of The Land of the Diamond Scarab!

And it was all done through voice alone.

Evidence

By this time, you may be wondering *why*. Creative drama takes time, whether in small bits interspersed in lessons or in whole sessions devoted to itself. What is the evidence that it is any good for anything, not least of all for teaching the language arts? To try to answer this question, I'll turn to three sources of evidence: the experts, the research, and *you*.

Experts. Mem Fox (1987) draws on her own vast experience to present song, movement, and story-enactment sessions based on "in-school trials and tribulations" in Australia. Her sessions highlight specific learnings in phonics, science, and understanding one's community. She asserts that drama includes all functions of language. She adds, "I think one of the loveliest advantages of drama is that it gives all children the chance to be successful" (p. 4). Heinig (1988) provides an experience-based book containing a drama sequence that can be adapted to almost any classroom, thus substantiating her claim that creative drama promotes language development, communication, problem solving, and creativity (pp. 5-13). Similar claims and cases appear in creative drama methods books by Stewig (1983), Siks (1983), and McCaslin (1990). At the height of the behaviorist movement, Shaw (1970) compiled a taxonomy of objectives attributed to creative drama, based on content analysis of experts' writings.

Research. Empirical studies that attempt to pin down the effects of drama in schools are summarized in articles by Vitz (1983), Wagner (1988), and Kardash and Wright (1987). Vitz found language arts instruction that favored drama over other treatments in 21 of 32 studies. The advantage of drama was greater for speaking and listening outcomes than for reading. Wagner reports generally favorable, but not consistent, results for drama. She noted improved language skills for low socioeconomic and English as a second language groups that participated in creative drama sessions, although not in all cases: in 2 of the 12 studies there were no such gains. Reading comprehension, at least in recall of story, generally improved through drama, though again such results were not found in all studies. Persuasive writing improved significantly as a result of creative drama involving role playing.

The meta-analysis of Kardash and Wright is most interesting. Taken together, the studies indicated that the effects of creative drama "can be expected to move the typical student from the 50th to the 75th percentile of the untreated population" (p. 15). But in what? Not consistently or dependably in reading, although in certain studies and on certain measures (for example, the Paragraph Meaning subtest on the Stanford Achievement Test) reading comprehension increased significantly for intermediate graders, as did reading readiness scores for kindergartners. More consistent evidence from the studies shows the positive effect of creative drama on "oral language skills, self-esteem, and moral reasoning skills" (p. 17). Kardash and Wright note a lack of information in reports of creative drama. What exactly was done and by whom? Only in one report were the sessions conducted by a drama specialist; interestingly, this study showed the largest positive effects.

There is a possibility that some of the gains in language arts achievement attributed to creative drama are a result of students' increased interest in what for many was a novel approach.

For this reason, Kardash and Wright recommend that studies be made in school systems where creative drama is ongoing and continuous, not devised as a short-term experimental treatment. Vitz has a different concern: the "anyone can do it syndrome" (p. 24), which may mean that some treatments involving creative drama suffered from inadequate leadership. (For a more comprehensive review of research on drama and its effect on oral language, reading, and writing, see Wagner, 1991, pp. 796-800.)

Your own evidence. In many ways, there's a fresh vision of what we want to attain in reading and the language arts. Reading scores on decoding and comprehension, whatever their validity, no longer seem adequate to assess a reading program. We also want to find out whether students like to read. Are they reading voluntarily? Are they seeking materials in a range of genres? Are they able to build mental imagery as they read? In writing, too, there's a fresh perspective. We no longer assess writing only by the mechanics and the ability to stick to a topic or theme; we now look at the way writers enter into the writing process, and the way they vary the "voice" in writing according to audience and language function. We worry about spelling, but the champions of emergent literacy have given us new ideas of how it develops and how to teach it. Perhaps a fresh vision of speech and listening will come. After all, most young people seem (to their elders) to talk plenty and even, at times, to listen. Yet the most comprehensive of recent reports on speaking and listening in the classroom (Pinnell & Jaggar, 1991) is rife with examples of the need to update and upgrade this area of the language arts.

I mention this fresh vision because it should influence you as you place creative drama in your lesson plans. Begin, in fact, by thinking not about what drama technique to try but about what language arts vision you want to attain. Here are examples of the sort of thoughts you might have:

- "I want my class to have a clearer image of the California Gold Rush. I want them to be able to write a better paragraph about it than the textbook contains. Then I want them to be able to fit it in when we web or outline the Westward expansion."

- "I want my students not to confine their free-choice reading to books that are about a roomful of themselves—either that or wild, irresponsible love and adventure. I'm glad they read something but I'd like to see them turn once in a while to social issues, to people not all like themselves, to a wider world."
- "I would like to give a purpose for speaking and writing other than journals."

When you have applied vision to the needs of your students, then consider whether and how creative drama techniques may help attain it. Select carefully and deliberately, using literature, content area topics, and real-life experiences as substance for brief explorations of direct POV, role playing, or extended sessions that include warm-ups, enactments, and evaluation.

Collect your own evidence. Videotaping, if feasible, can show progress from first excursions into drama into later sessions. Anecdotes jotted down, dated, and placed in a folder can give evidence of progress. Students' reading logs can help you look for evidence of increased amount and variety of genres in free-choice reading. Ask students themselves to find evidence of the effects of creative drama on their language arts.

Does it work? Does it bring more than excitement? Motivation? Inspiration? Does it improve skills? Does it relate oracy and literacy more powerfully to our lives? Your own evidence is, ultimately, your best guide to the relationship of creative drama to the language arts.

References

*Fox, M. (1987). *Teaching drama to young children*. Portsmouth, NH: Heinemann.

Heath, S.B. (1982). What no bedtime story means: Narrative skills at home and school. *Language in Society, 11*, 49-76.

*Heinig, R.B. (1988). *Creative drama for the classroom teacher* (3rd ed.). Englewood Cliffs, NJ: Prentice Hall.

Johnson, L., & O'Neill, C. (Eds.). (1984). *Dorothy Heathcote: Collected writings on education and drama*. London: Hutchinson.

Kardash, C.A.M., & Wright, L. (1987). Does creative drama benefit elementary school students: A meta-analysis. *Youth Theater Journal, 2*, 11-18.

*McCaslin, N. (1990). *Creative drama in the classroom* (5th ed.). White Plains, NY: Longman.

Pinnell, G.S., & Jaggar, A.M. (1991). Oral language: Speaking and listening in the classroom. In J. Flood, J.M. Jensen, D. Lapp, & J.R. Squire (Eds.), *Handbook of research on teaching the English language arts* (pp. 691-719). New York: Macmillan.

Sebesta, S.L., & Monson, D.L. (1992, March). *Basal readers and the aesthetic stance.* Paper presented at the WORD Research Conference, Tacoma, WA.

Shaw, A.M. (1970). A taxonomical study of the nature and behavioral objectives of creative drama. *Educational Theatre Journal, 22,* 361-372.

*Siks, G.B. (1983). *Drama with children* (2nd ed.). New York: HarperCollins.

*Spolin, V. (1986). *Theater games for the classroom: A teacher's handbook.* Evanston, IL: Northwestern University Press.

*Stewig, J.W. (1983). *Informal drama in the elementary language arts program.* New York: Teachers College Press.

Vitz, K. (1983). A review of empirical research in drama and language. *Children's Theatre Review, 32,* 17-25.

Wagner, B.J. (1988). Research currents: Does classroom drama affect the arts of language? *Language Arts, 65,* 46-51.

Wagner, B.J. (1991). Imaginative expression. In J. Flood, J.M. Jensen, D. Lapp, & J.R. Squire (Eds.), *Handbook of research on teaching the English language arts* (pp. 787-804). New York: Macmillan.

* indicates a book with rationale and teaching ideas for creative drama.

Children's Books

Adorjan, C., & Rasovsky, Y. (1988). *WKID: Easy radio plays.* Niles, IL: Whitman.

Allard, H. (1991). *The cactus flower bakery.* (Ill. by N. Delaney.) New York: HarperCollins.

Avi. (1991). *Nothing but the truth: A documentary novel.* New York: Orchard.

Avi. (1992). *"Who was that masked man, anyway?".* New York: Orchard.

Burnett, F.H. (1987). *The secret garden.* New York: Grosset & Dunlap. (Original work published 1911)

Charles, D. (1992). *Chancay and the secret of fire: A Peruvian folktale.* New York: Whitebird/Putnam.

Delton, J. (1992). *Lights, action, land-ho!* (Pee Wee Scouts series; ill. by A. Tiegreen.) New York: Dell.

Demi. (1991). *The artist and the architect.* New York: Henry Holt.

Freedman, R. (1991). *The Wright Brothers: How they invented the airplane.* New York: Holiday House.

Kimmel, E.A. (Reteller). (1988). *Anansi and the moss-covered rock.* (Ill. by J. Stevens.) New York: Holiday House.

Kimmel, E.A. (Reteller). (1992). *Anansi goes fishing.* (Ill. by J. Stevens.) New York: Holiday House.

Kline, S. (1992). *The Herbie Jones reader's theater*. New York: Putnam.

Namioka, L. (1992). *Yang the youngest and his terrible ear*. (Ill. by K. de Kiefte.) Boston, MA: Little, Brown.

Paterson, K. (1991). *Lyddie*. New York: Lodestar/Dutton.

Steptoe, J. (1987). *Mufaro's beautiful daughters: An African tale*. New York: Lothrop, Lee & Shepard.

Wyman, A. (1991). *Red sky at morning*. New York: Holiday House.

Chapter 4

"It's Really Special because You Get to Think": Talking about Literature

Julie E. Wollman-Bonilla

leven-year-old Dawn explained how important talk is for making sense of literature when I interviewed her about the literature-group discussions in her combined fifth/sixth grade classroom:

> The technique that we are using with the books...it's really special because you get to think, and I think it teaches us a lot about books instead of the other way where you have to answer questions.
>
> You really have to listen to what other people say so that you can understand the book.... I listen to what other people

say so I can get an idea of what they thought about it, and I listen to their questions to see if I agree with them. I like to add to what people say and I like to get in my own comments to see what other people will think.... If I say something and they don't add on to it but they say, "I disagree because so-and-so," I may change my mind or I may still disagree.... You learn what they think about it and what they think about what you said.

Sometimes I start to say something but then I stop 'cause if I don't understand what I'm talking about nobody else will.... So I do kind of learn about what I think.

Dawn's teacher began the year using basal readers and following the lessons outlined in the accompanying teacher's manual, but she sensed students were as bored with this approach as she was. Intrigued by the idea of using real literature and becoming a facilitator and participant rather than a controller of classroom talk, she organized literature groups in late fall. When I interviewed Dawn she had been involved in such groups for several months.

Dawn suggests that discussing a book in a small group helps her think more deeply and develop greater understanding about what she reads than she did when she worked alone to answer predetermined questions. Talking with others forces her to organize her thoughts so they can be communicated clearly, allows her to try out her ideas and get feedback, introduces her to new perspectives and information, and encourages collaborative sense-making. This is possible, Dawn explains, because the teacher "is not really in charge of the group," and because exploratory talk is the norm in her classroom.

In this chapter I build on Dawn's comments to explore the value of discussing books, outline qualities of successful literature discussions, and provide specific examples of how students grow in literacy through participation in literature groups. I have drawn on my observations of literature discussions involving students from diverse ethnic and socioeconomic backgrounds in regular, special education, and remedial programs from kindergarten to sixth grade.

"I learn about what I think":
Talk as a Tool for Learning

Talk is more than a way to communicate or transmit information; it is a powerful tool for thinking (Edwards & Westgate, 1987). Talk is powerful not only because we as individuals use language to think, but also because we learn through social interaction (Vygotsky, 1962, 1978). Collaboration to solve problems and make sense of new information is supported by talk. And, because as we talk we become aware of what we think and know and wonder about, talk provides the foundation on which we can build by relating new information to existing knowledge and ideas.

Theory and research suggest that talk helps learners recognize and clarify their ideas, introduces them to new perspectives, and facilitates reflection and innovative thinking (Barnes, 1975, 1976; Britton, 1970, 1982). Rosenblatt (1938) has long argued that collaborative discussions of literature involving students and teacher can support and challenge readers in their sense-making efforts. Researchers who have studied these "reader response" groups describe how the meanings group members construct together may not match the understanding the individuals would have come to alone (Bleich, 1986; Fish, 1980; Golden, 1987; Hepler & Hickman, 1982; Rosenblatt, 1985). This applies to teachers and students alike, for when teachers are true collaborators in small groups, their perspectives become negotiable—just like everyone else's.

Collaborative talk that helps learners make sense of specific texts—and of life in general—and deepens their understanding of and appreciation for literature is more like informal, everyday conversation than traditional teacher-dominated lessons. In order to facilitate conversational discourse, classrooms must be supportive environments where students' knowledge is recognized and appreciated, students' voices are valued, and exploratory talk is encouraged. Teachers play a crucial role in creating contexts in which all students feel entitled to participate and responsible for sharing their ideas and asking their questions.

"I like to get in my own comments":
Making Literature Discussions Work

Successful literature discussions characterized by the learning tool of informal talk share certain qualities, regardless of the nature of the setting or the participants. These qualities are, in large part, a result of how teachers organize and participate in the discussions.

First, teachers establish that literature discussions are a place to discuss books, not to compete with displays of reading ability or speed. Students are given time to read and, in some classrooms, write down their responses and questions before their group meeting (Wollman-Bonilla, 1991a). They are not asked to read aloud during meetings. One sixth grader who participated in a group in which the teacher required reading aloud explained to me, "I just get nervous and mess up" when his turn to read came around. His fear of embarrassing himself led to general discomfort with the group meetings, which resulted in his being hesitant to contribute *any* ideas during literature-group discussions. His peers shared his uncertainty and their group meetings never grew into collaborative discussions. Of course, students sometimes choose to read from the text to support a comment or opinion, but it is preferable that teachers never require reading aloud.

Second, teachers participate as students' equals in terms of knowledge and right to the floor. Instead of dominating the discourse, asking a lot of test-like questions, and evaluating students' contributions, teachers listen more, talk less, and do not pretend to be experts. Teachers encourage students to ask their questions and share their ideas. When teachers do participate, they contribute authentically, asking questions that are genuine requests for information and expressing uncertainty or confusion when puzzled. By refusing to judge students' contributions, teachers establish that there is no one, predetermined right answer or best interpretation. Literature discussions thereby become safe places to try out ideas with the knowledge that whatever is said will be listened to and respected.

Third, teachers model exploratory, collaborative talk. By thinking aloud, listening with interest, and responding to children's comments with their own opinions or observations, teachers model how to contribute ideas and give helpful feedback. Teachers' responses demonstrate that collaborators respect one another's ideas and question and challenge one another intellectually, not personally. When participants believe that group members value their ideas and will not attack them personally, even reticent, uncertain students find their voices.

Fourth, the teacher is aware that the group meanings are constructed together by all group members. Students bring to the classroom diverse "values, beliefs," and "attitudes" (Gee, 1989, pp. 6-7) that may not match teachers' perspectives on literacy and instruction (Heath, 1983). For example, some students might hesitate to speak out in discussions with an adult because this would be considered inappropriate behavior in their homes or communities (see, for example, Scollon & Scollon, 1981; Wollman-Bonilla, 1991b). Some students feel that relating literature to their own experiences is an appropriate way to respond to reading, while others feel that literature discussions should stay close to the text (see, for example, Miller, Nemoianu, & DeJong, 1986; Wollman-Bonilla, 1991b). Students' beliefs about classroom interaction and reading necessarily shape what happens when they meet for discussions.

Teachers can help establish the value of students' contributions and can encourage them to share their ideas by recognizing and acknowledging students' different perspectives and norms for interaction. Understanding and respecting these differences entails listening to students, assuming that they are curious and have knowledge to share even if they are silent, and asking them to talk about their assumptions and expectations (Wollman-Bonilla, 1991b). Even young students can explain what they view as appropriate classroom behavior. Teachers can sometimes restructure literature discussions to create contexts in which students feel comfortable talking. Teachers might choose to assign a student leader and participate themselves only as listeners, or they may ask students to meet for discussion on their own and rejoin the group once students are comfortable voicing their ideas. Asking students to choose the text for discussion is often beneficial for encouraging talk, because if students view the reading as germane to their lives or interests, they will be more likely to get involved in discussions about it. And, of course, teachers must always listen for the logic and relevance in students' contributions and build on students' intentions, even if their comments initially appear to be unrelated to the topic under discussion.

Fifth, teachers explicitly state their goals and expectations for how students will participate, rather than assuming these are understood. This step is particularly important in classrooms where norms for interaction are not shared. Conflicting assumptions often make students appear to know—or care—less than they really do, because they do not know how to participate in the way the teacher expects.

Consider an example of one discussion group in a sixth grade classroom. Before they began meeting, the students in this group said they believed that the teacher was the expert who could tell them "what it means and how it is." They agreed that it was more important to listen to the teacher than to listen to their peers or to share their own ideas. In addition, these students were very concerned with how the teacher would evaluate their work and sought to please him and avoid saying anything that would make them appear "dumb." They looked to the teacher to lead literature-group meetings as if they were teacher-directed lessons; he never explicitly said he did not want to play this role.

The teacher interpreted students' resulting hesitance to participate voluntarily as an indication that they had nothing to say. Despite his desire to facilitate discussion, he felt he had to dominate and direct the discourse. The students, on the other hand, were frustrated. They believed they should have *some* opportunity to ask and answer questions, but the teacher seemed always to be talking—often answering his own questions before students had a chance to venture in with their thoughts. Ironically, in his effort to "cover" for students' uncertainty about informal discussions with a teacher, the teacher failed to acknowledge and build on students' desire to participate. Such misunderstanding about expectations contributes to the creation of an environment that greatly inhibits collaborative talk.

Finally, teachers invite students to create guidelines for the literature discussions. In one second grade classroom, for example, the teacher had trouble guiding students to listen and respond to one another until she asked them to talk about why they were meeting in small groups and what they might be learning from one another. Based on this discussion, the students then came up with some purposes and corresponding "rules" for group meetings, which they talked about, revised, and made into a wall chart. One fifth/sixth grade teacher also invited students to solve a common problem by discussing it:

> Teacher: Anybody want to offer an opinion as to how they want to proceed for the rest of this book—and for the future books? Do you want me to give you a kind of schedule where by a certain date you should finish it...or what?

> Mira: I think you should give us a date to finish one chapter, so that we can all be in the same chapter...'cause if people go further some people will be finished the book and they won't be interested in it anymore and they'll just be telling everybody what's going on and what's gonna be happening.

> Abby: Yeah, when people keep on waiting for other people it's gonna be boring then, so we should keep a date for when the whole chapter or the whole book should be finished.

> Oscar: Well, what about we should have a certain amount of the chapter to read one day, then the next day....

> Abby: I like reading from chapter four to six or something. Reading a chapter at a time is kind of boring.

> Oscar: Yeah, 'cause you lose the point by the time you get to the next chapter....

When everyone had shared his or her opinions on how to structure the reading assignments, the teacher said, "So, at the end of the sessions today, perhaps we could find a goal and decide when we should finish."

Student participation in making the "rules" for literature discussions helps clarify the purpose and procedures for the group meetings, signals that students share control of what happens, and gives students an investment in making it work.

"The technique we are using teaches us a lot": Students' Growth in Literacy

In the collaborative discussions of literature-group meetings, students learn reading strategies, they learn about literature, they work together to construct meaning, and they learn to value and share personal responses. Students are able to construct a richer understanding of specific texts—and ultimately of life—by using the knowledge and abilities they develop to read more efficiently, deeply, and critically. Teachers participate as equals in these groups and, by doing so, create a context in which many opportunities exist for supporting and assessing students' developing reading, speaking, listening, and thinking strategies in meaningful ways.

Learning reading strategies. One of the benefits of collaborative discussions of literature is that from them students learn strategies for solving reading problems and constructing meaning. Good readers make sense of texts by forming hypotheses and then confirming or correcting these as they go along (Goodman, 1984; Smith, 1982). They engage in this process by drawing on two sources of information: the text itself and their background knowledge.

Through participation in literature discussions students learn to use texts to get information that helps them construct meaning. Some students may already have control of this strategy—they may consciously use texts to find answers to their questions, and they may back up what they say with text evidence. Boris, a sixth grader, modeled this strategy when he described Tom Sawyer by saying, "This kid is lazy. I say that because it's like he's 'oh hum de dum dum dum' while this other kid is doing all the work." Comments such as this show how textual information can lend validity to a contribution and can aid in developing understanding of characters and events. When Boris said, "I say that because..." he was explicitly stating that he draws on text evidence to verify his observations.

Teachers can also model how to use texts to form hypotheses and solve problems. For example, openly struggling with the language of Ernest J. Gaines's *The Autobiography of Miss Jane Pittman*, one teacher, with support from his students, articulated how he figured out that a "gallery" is a porch:

> Teacher: This is the second time that Jane's referred to the gallery.
>
> Amy: Is that like a porch?
>
> Teacher: I think it's exactly like a porch. At first I thought it might have been the kitchen.
>
> Jacob: Yeah.
>
> Teacher: But from this description—"standing outside..."
>
> Amy (joining in): "...outside the..."
>
> Teacher: Exactly.
>
> Lynette: It's like a brick porch.

Teachers can reinforce the use of this strategy by asking students in literature discussions to find and state evidence for their hypotheses or to look to the text to clarify confusion or answer questions. Requests that students try to use the text, and explicit displays of how to do so, create a context in which students can see how this strategy works and practice using it. Those who are unfamiliar with the strategy can draw on peer and teacher models and can count on the support of the group as they try it out.

Another tool for making meaning is the use of background knowledge. Reading relies on all sorts of background knowledge that readers bring to texts, including general knowledge of language and of the world, along with readers' own specific, personal experiences. Often the relationship between a reader's experiences and the text is what gives meaning and significance to the reading. Although teachers may worry that students are moving too far from the text when they introduce and elaborate on background knowledge in literature discussions, in fact this is a sophisticated and useful strategy. A direct connection to the text almost always becomes evident when students are given attention and time to complete and articulate their thoughts.

Many students naturally relate their own experiences and what they see on television, in movies, and in their own communities to what they read; some make connections to other texts or earlier sections in the text they are reading. In literature discussions teachers can participate in modeling and reinforcing the use of background knowledge to solve reading problems. For example, during a discussion of *The Autobiography of Miss Jane Pittman* Jacob asked, "Wasn't it illegal to kill blacks just because they were black?" Others in the group agreed that this was puzzling since there was a law against racially motivated violence but "the whites did it anyway." The teacher drew on his background knowledge to respond:

> Teacher: Well, there's lots of laws, and there's lots of people who don't obey them.
>
> Amy: Just like the people who...break into places.
>
> Teacher: Crack is illegal. Selling crack is illegal.
>
> Amir: They still do it though.

Teachers can also *ask* students to connect what they are reading with their background knowledge during literature discussions. For example, a group of fifth and sixth graders was reading Katherine Paterson's *Bridge to Terabithia*. Several students were puzzled by the "big gap" between chapters that makes it seem like "the year goes so fast." After some discussion the teacher asked, "Is that unusual? When you think about some of the books you've read, is it unusual to jump ahead that quickly?" The group talked about this question and then moved to a discussion of movies they had seen that skipped long periods of time. Based on their discussion, they decided that authors need to focus on key events instead of trying to cover every small detail, otherwise their books would be long and boring.

As when they look to the text for information, students'
and teachers' use of background knowledge to solve problems
serve as demonstrations of the strategy and help establish it as a
valuable tool. Responding to a call for background knowledge and
building on other group members' use of it are safe ways for all
students to try out this strategy.

Learning about literature. Knowledge of literature is actually a particular type of background knowledge. Often during literature discussions students contribute observations about an
author's use of literary techniques or devices. For example, they
may argue about whose point of view is being presented or over-
looked, or comment on choices the author has made—as the students who wondered about the "gap" in *Bridge to Terabithia* did.
Teachers and peers can elaborate on these comments to help group
members develop awareness of the wider significance of the literary techniques they noticed. Consider this exchange from a sixth
grade group that was discussing Mark Twain's *The Adventures of
Tom Sawyer*:

> Carlos: It's boring. It ain't like a chapter with him
> always doing something. Here all he was doing
> was thinking of trying to do something. But he
> wasn't gonna do it.
>
> Teacher: You're saying that a lot of the chapter takes place
> in Tom Sawyer's head, in his mind, where he's
> thinking about....
>
> Julia: Yeah.
>
> Lynette: Yeah, but it shows the sentimental part of him.
> He's not always a bad little boy.

Carlos alluded to two common modes of plot development: presenting action and describing characters' thoughts. The teacher
labeled the technique Carlos observed and, building on this
exchange, Lynette argued that there is a purpose to the author's
focusing on Tom's thoughts.

Another example demonstrates how teachers and peers can
remind the group that there is an author—and a plan—behind the

text. The group reading *Bridge to Terabithia* had a long discussion of how rapidly the book seemed to end, leaving problems unsettled and the reader wondering what happened to many of the characters. Building on students' comments, the teacher joined in the discussion:

> Teacher: Why do you think she might have ended it that way?
>
> Dawn: Maybe because authors sometimes like to make you get into it, make you ask, like, "What else could happen?"
>
> Jasmine: Maybe she wants to keep us in suspense but there's no other thing, like if one chapter is really good and you want to go on to the next chapter really fast and you have to stop, and you say, "Oh, I wanna read the next chapter," then you can, then that's a reason. You wanna put them in suspense and make them read on more.

The teacher's question encouraged Dawn to articulate her awareness that literary texts sometimes end with a lot of questions because this keeps the reader involved in thinking about what might come next. Jasmine argued that the reason for such an abrupt ending could not be to "make you get into it" because the book ends—the author is no longer trying to keep the reader from putting the book down. In the process of explaining her opinion, she explicitly shared her knowledge of the literary technique of creating suspense. This sharing may have helped other group members learn about the technique or extend their understanding of how it works, all in the context of a real problem raised by the students.

Teachers can also use literature discussions to introduce literary devices purposefully. For example, when students were shocked and dismayed at Leslie's death in *Bridge to Terabithia*, the teacher recognized an opportunity to introduce the technique of foreshadowing in a meaningful way:

> Mira: She was perfectly healthy; she did so many things great, you know. She was like a perfect athlete.

Teacher: What about the days before her death—weren't you getting some kind of "dark clouds"? What was taking place in the week of vacation? What was happening that week to kind of spoil the mood?

The students talked at length about the chapter preceding Leslie's death, which describes a week-long storm, Jess's growing fear of crossing the rain-swelled creek, and his hesitance to share his fear with Leslie. The teacher then guided students to take a new perspective on what many initially thought was a "worthless and boring" chapter by considering exactly how it foreshadowed Leslie's death.

By building on topics raised in literature discussions, students and teachers collaborate to share and develop their knowledge of literary techniques through their talk. Learning about literature helps students in reading, and it also helps them recognize that authors are real people who sometimes make imperfect decisions. Demystifying authorship and discussing the kinds of choices authors make and the techniques they use can also help students with *their* writing.

Making meaning together. In literature discussions, each group collaborates to solve problems that are of interest or concern to group members. The meanings that emerge from each group's thinking together are often better developed and more comprehensive than the understanding individuals construct on their own. These meanings might even extend beyond the text and help group members make sense of their lives and the world around them.

In one group, for example, students had finished *Bridge to Terabithia* and were talking about their reactions to Jess making his sister, May Belle, the queen of Terabithia in place of Leslie. Dawn was curious about why Jess chose May Belle and began to articulate a question:

Dawn: I wanna know if Jess just picked May Belle to be queen because...uh....

Jasmine: There wasn't anybody else.

> Dawn: When she followed Jess and knew about it, I want to know if that had to do with it.... And how she followed him and...she didn't.... I don't know, but I just think that maybe he picked her because....
>
> Mira: She already knew about it.
>
> Dawn: She already knew about it. Right.
>
> Alonso: I think it's also that May Belle already knew about it. So I think that he picked her about that. Also that May Belle respected Jess, even though there were some fights or arguments. That's common in between brothers and sisters.

The conversation continued with Mira elaborating on Alonso's comment, observing that even when Jess got angry and slapped May Belle, she didn't stay mad at him for long. Together, Jasmine, Mira, and Alonso built on Dawn's question to construct a group understanding of why Jess picked May Belle as queen and of sibling relationships in general.

In this process of meaning construction through talk, teachers' contributions are on an equal footing with students'. For example, the students in one group disagreed when discussing the section of *The Autobiography of Miss Jane Pittman* in which Jane encounters an old man who tries to guide her north. Some students argued that she was stupid to ignore the man's advice because she was desperate for help; others said she was just being cautious. The teacher suggested that Jane wasn't necessarily stupid but rather uneducated—"She's an 11-year-old who never spent a day in school." Several students insisted this was another reason she should listen to the man. The teacher again tried to introduce his interpretation of Jane's "stupidity":

> Teacher: Does she strike you as the type of person who, if she had gone to school from first grade, would know this stuff?
>
> Amir: Yeah.

Teacher: So, is there a difference between someone who's stupid and someone who hasn't had a chance to learn? Or is it the same, in your opinion? Is she a stupid person or is she just a person who's never had an opportunity to learn?

Lynette agreed that Jane had never had the opportunity to learn, but felt her problem was that "she doesn't let nobody help her." Others in the group agreed that there was no reason for the man to mislead her and that Jane should have known that, despite her lack of schooling. This group-constructed interpretation of Jane's motivations was not congruent with the interpretation the teacher suggested, yet it seemed to be accepted by all at the end of the discussion.

This is not to suggest that collaborative sense-making in literature discussions always leads—or should lead—to an answer or agreement. Sometimes group members work together to articulate problems or concerns that have no simple solutions or are open to many interpretations. By working together to solve problems and share ideas and by listening to one anothers' opinions, however, students come to recognize and respect a range of perspectives. As a result, group members develop deeper understanding and new ways of thinking—about texts, themselves, their peers, and life in general.

Learning to value and share personal responses. Students may be moved, entertained, angered, or bored by what they read. Encouraging students to share personal responses during literature discussions allows them to relive the pleasure they experienced while reading or to articulate and sort through disturbing or unhappy reactions to texts. Providing the opportunity to air dissatisfaction with a text is also important, not only because it lets students know that their feelings and opinions matter but also because voicing criticism may relieve anger or boredom. As one student said, "You get frustrated" if you can't say what you really think. When they talk about literature-group discussions, students express their belief in the value of "giving your own opinions" and not being constrained by predetermined questions.

Often students spontaneously share their personal responses, as in this example from a discussion focused on *Tom Sawyer*:

Gabriel: Huck is really spoiled. He can do anything he wants, whenever he wants.

Boris: Well, how would you like it—not having any parents?

Gabriel: You wouldn't have to do anything. It would be fun.

Lynette: I kinda think he's disgusting. I mean he doesn't wash or nothing, and he stays in the same clothes....

These personal responses brought a variety of perspectives to the group and led to a discussion of Huck's living situation. Students' questions were answered and the group constructed a clearer understanding of Huck's life and, all things considered, how they felt about him.

Sometimes the process of sharing a personal response leads to deeper understanding because, through talk, students reflect on how a text aroused certain feelings and prompted reactions. For example, as Alonso described the evolution of his feelings about Leslie's death in *Bridge to Terabithia*, he recognized that those feelings had changed with the book's and Jess's moods:

It weared off.... At first Jess was sad that Leslie died—that was a tremendous hit for Jess and for us, the reader. But then they started talking about nicer things and so you, like, it feels like if it's wearing off.

Personal responses may be so powerful and spontaneous that students can't wait until literature-group meetings to express them. The morning after Mira read that Leslie had died, the first thing she said to her teacher was "I'm not reading this book anymore." When her group met, she blurted out, "I didn't want that to happen." Her teacher, believing that it would be valuable for the entire group to hear Mira's initial, stronger response, said, "It really hit me when Mira said to me this morning, 'I'm not reading this book anymore.' Would you like to explain your feelings?" With these words the teacher described how Mira's strong reaction deepened her own response, signaled that personal responses are valuable, and invited Mira to share her response with the group.

By encouraging and validating group members' personal responses, teachers and peers help students value those responses and develop their capacity for responding through demonstrations and practice during discussions. In addition, personal responses provide a way into the text and are often the impetus for productive sense-making discussions in which students build a deeper understanding of their reading.

A context for authentic assessment. Just as students learn from one another during literature discussions, teachers also discover new ways of thinking about texts and come to appreciate new perspectives. At the same time, listening to the talk of literature groups is useful as a means of authentic assessment. Students often display their best thinking during group discussions. In this informal, supportive context, they are more likely to contribute and to share their ideas fully, without fear of embarrassment or error.

As the samples of dialogue I have included illustrate, students' comments reveal how they approach and understand texts. Teachers who participate in literature discussions gather information about students' attitudes toward reading, use of reading strategies, approaches to meaning construction, and personal engagement with texts. This type of information can serve as a guide in choosing texts and designing reading activities and can suggest ways that teachers might participate in discussions and work with students individually to address weaknesses and celebrate and enhance strengths.

"It's really special": The Many Benefits of Literature Discussion

Students grow in literacy, learn important information about reading, and develop knowledge about texts and life through collaborative discussion of literature. However, students also benefit from literature discussions in other ways: for example, they discover the value and pleasure of working together, and perhaps most significant, they develop new habits of mind—they come to think more critically and creatively. Just as students who regularly share their writing begin to anticipate and address the questions and challenges readers might pose (Calkins, 1986), students who participate in literature discussions begin to reflect on and polish their ideas about their reading, as if they are imagining others' reactions. As Dawn said, "Sometimes I start to say something but then I stop 'cause if I don't understand what I'm talking about, nobody else will." Dawn's critical awareness of her own thinking and her challenging of herself reflect sophisticated abilities that develop naturally as students participate in literature discussions.

References

Barnes, D. (1975). *From communication to curriculum.* New York: Penguin.

Barnes, D. (1976). Language strategies in learning. In M. Torbe & R. Protherough (Eds.), *Classroom encounters: Language and English teaching* (pp. 155-159). London: Ward Lock Educational and the National Association for the Teaching of English.

Bleich, D. (1986). Cognitive stereoscopy and the study of language and literature. In B.T. Petersen (Ed.), *Convergences: Transactions in reading and writing* (pp. 99-114). Urbana, IL: National Council of Teachers of English.

Britton, J. (1970). *Language and learning.* New York: Penguin.

Britton, J. (1982). *Prospect and retrospect: Selected essays of James Britton.* Montclair, NJ: Boynton/Cook.

Calkins, L.M. (1986). *The art of teaching writing.* Portsmouth, NH: Heinemann.

Edwards, D., & Westgate, D.P.G. (1987). *Investigating classroom talk.* Philadelphia, PA: Falmer.

Fish, S. (1980). *Is there a text in this class? The authority of interpretive communities.* Cambridge, MA: Harvard University Press.

Gee, J.P. (1989). Literacy, discourse, and linguistics: Introduction. *Journal of Education, 171,* 5-25.

Golden, J.M. (1987). An exploration of reader-text interaction in a small group discussion. In D. Bloome (Ed.), *Literacy and schooling* (pp. 169-192). Norwood, NJ: Ablex.

Goodman, K.S. (1984). The reading process: Theory and practice. In R.E. Hodges & E.H. Rudorf (Eds.), *Language and learning to read: What teachers should know about language* (pp. 141-159). New York: University Press of America.

Heath, S.B. (1983). *Ways with words: Language, life, and work in communities and classrooms.* Cambridge, UK: Cambridge University Press.

Hepler, S.I., & Hickman, J. (1982). "The book was okay. I love you"—Social aspects of response to literature. *Theory into Practice, 21,* 278-283.

Miller, P., Nemoianu, A., & DeJong, J. (1986). Early reading at home: Its practice and meanings in a working-class community. In B.B. Schieffelin & P. Gilmore (Eds.), *The acquisition of literacy: Ethnographic perspectives* (pp. 132-154). Norwood, NJ: Ablex.

Rosenblatt, L.M. (1938). *Literature as exploration*. New York: Appleton-Century.

Rosenblatt, L.M. (1985). Viewpoints: Transaction versus interaction—A terminological rescue operation. *Research in the Teaching of English, 19*, 96-107.

Scollon, R., & Scollon, S.B.K. (1981). *Narrative, literacy, and face in interethnic communication*. Norwood, NJ: Ablex.

Smith, F. (1982). *Understanding reading: A psycholinguistic analysis of learning to read* (3rd ed.). New York: Holt, Rinehart & Winston.

Vygotsky, L.S. (1962). *Thought and language* (E. Hanfmann & G. Vakar, Trans. and Eds.). Cambridge, MA: M.I.T. Press.

Vygotsky, L.S. (1978). *Mind in society: The development of higher psychological processes* (M. Cole, V. John-Steiner, S. Scribner, & E. Souberman, Eds.). Cambridge, MA: Harvard University Press.

Wollman-Bonilla, J.E. (1991a). *Response journals: Inviting students to think and write about literature*. New York: Scholastic.

Wollman-Bonilla, J.E. (1991b). *Discourse practices and the social construction of meaning in small group literature discussions among sixth graders and their teacher*. Unpublished doctoral dissertation, New York University, New York, NY.

Children's Books

Gaines, E.J. (1971). *The autobiography of Miss Jane Pittman*. New York: Dial.

Paterson, K. (1977). *Bridge to Terabithia*. New York: Crowell.

Twain, M. (1972). *The adventures of Tom Sawyer*. New York: Washington Square. (Original work published 1876)

Chapter 5

Literature Circles:
Hearing Children's Voices

Kathy G. Short
Charlene Klassen

I nstead of starting this chapter with a discussion of the theoretical rationale for and a practical definition of "literature circles," we want you to hear the powerful voices of children:

> There is this thing called literature circles. And that is something where you're in a group with three or four other people. I read a book and then I discuss what the meaning is and what role did the characters play.
>
> *Corey, grade three*

> In first and second grade, we did skill packs and if we did not know the answer we would tell the teacher and she would say, "Read this paragraph and you will find the answer." And now

we have literature circles and people push you if you don't talk. And that way we learn more.

Nicole, grade three

Literature circles take the ideas out of your head rather than keeping all the ideas in your head. In literature circles, you get to know a person better and how that book relates to their life and how you and them relate.

Jamie, grade three

When I am in a literature group, I feel I am growing a lot in being able to understand the deep-down meaning of the book and how the author wrote that book.

Carl, grade three

Here everybody is equal. We can all read books and talk about them with each other. Some people might take longer to read a book but everybody does it and everybody has something to say. We all get more ideas.

Jamie, grade three

I've changed because now I say what I want to say and not what the teacher wants me to say.

Megan, grade three

These children have experienced a classroom in which they are able to talk with others about their lived-through experiences with literature. For them, reading is a transaction, a process in which they actively construct understanding by bringing meaning to as well as taking meaning from a text (Rosenblatt, 1978). Their focus is not on extracting information from text or figuring out the interpretation they believe the teacher wants to hear. Instead, these children enter the world of fiction and nonfiction to learn about life and make sense of their own experiences and feelings. They bring their tentative understandings of the books they read to a literature circle, where they share their experiences with one another. As they talk, they examine their differing interpretations of the books they have read and come to new and deeper understandings of them.

Literature circles offer readers the opportunity to become literate. We want our students not only to love reading but also to think actively and critically about what they read. In literature circles, readers become critical thinkers as they engage in ongoing dialogue about their reading. The openness and depth of the literature circle discussions are possible because these students work in a collaborative community of learners. They have learned to trust one another and to engage in the give and take of collaboration—in literature circles and in all of their classroom life. The children's voices are heard and valued for their diversity. Both the teacher and the children attempt to really listen to one another because they realize that by doing so they will hear many new perspectives and push their own thinking. Learners come to know and value their own voices as well as those of their classmates. They examine their understandings and consider other ways of thinking about the world.

The intensive exploration that occurs in literature circles is only one of many ways these children experience literature in their classroom. They have extensive opportunities to read and enjoy books without having to write a report or have a discussion; they also listen to many books read aloud by their teacher and classmates and discuss these books in class. Throughout the day they use literature for meaningful purposes—such as for enjoyment or to learn something—not just to "practice" reading. Literature is integrated across the curriculum and is not relegated only to "reading time." It is out of this broad reading of many books for many reasons that a few books are chosen to be read and experienced more intensely in literature circles.

While literature circles in different classrooms share certain characteristics, there are a variety of ways in which they can be organized and integrated into the curriculum. In the first part of this chapter, we explore the many options for using literature circles in a classroom setting. We then share two examples of how literature circles work as part of broader inquiry studies within a classroom.

Looking at Options

It is impossible to describe one "right" way to set up literature circles. We have learned that there are many decisions teachers and students need to make as they organize for these discussions. While these decisions are neither right nor wrong, they do make a difference in the kind of talk that occurs in the groups (Hanssen, 1990). In this section, we describe the major decisions that teachers and students might consider and the implications of those decisions for classroom talk.

Focus of the Literature Circle

For many of the elementary teachers who first began exploring literature circles, literature was seen as a way to learn language, particularly reading and writing (Calkins, 1990; Goodman, 1988). The discussions in their classrooms tended to focus on the reading strategies students were using as they read different kinds of literature or on authors' writing styles and approaches to the writing process.

Some teachers also saw literature as a vehicle for learning other content (Edelsky, Altwerger, & Flores, 1990; Short & Armstrong, 1993). They organized their literature circles around themes and topics that were part of studies in science, history, mathematics, and so on. Discussion often focused on what was being learned about the topic through literature, and how that learning compared to learning from other sources.

Other teachers realized that literature study is a content area that provides a way of knowing that differs from other content areas (Peterson & Eeds, 1990; Smith, 1990). Through literature, readers experience life in a different way by living inside a story world (Rosenblatt, 1978). Discussion in these teachers' classrooms focused on lived-through experiences with texts and on the literary and artistic devices used by authors, illustrators, and readers to create these experiences.

More recently teachers have begun exploring literature as a way of learning about social, political, and cultural issues. Literature circles in their classrooms examined the complexities of students' own histories in light of the sociopolitical and cultural experiences depicted in literature. Through literature students can explore such issues as racism, homelessness, and conflict and get a greater sense of the complexities of the modern world.

Obviously these perspectives on literature and literature circles are not mutually exclusive, and all are usually present in any discussion. The perspective that is highlighted, however, will change the focus of the discussion and influence the circle's organization and the literature chosen. If the focus is on literature as a way to learn language, for example, literature circles might be organized around author studies and literature in which the characters use reading and writing as part of their daily lives. In any classroom, literature circles should emphasize all of these different perspectives over time to meet children's needs in making sense of the world.

Group Membership

The number of members in a literature circle has an impact on discussion because size creates different group dynamics and opportunities for talk. Some teachers have the whole class read the same book and move back and forth between small-group and whole-class discussions of it. This makes many perspectives on the book available and demonstrates to more hesitant class members a variety of ways to discuss literature. Working in whole-class groups, however, often means that fewer voices are heard and students have little or no choice about the literature that is read and discussed.

Literature circles are usually small groups of four or five students, although some teachers prefer groups of six or seven (Hanssen, 1990). Small groups allow students to choose the literature they will read and discuss. Members have more opportunities to talk and collaborate. When the groups finish their discussions, they can share with the class and thereby interest others in their books.

A third option is to read and discuss in pairs. In this case, interactions are more intense because both readers must be actively involved; of course, fewer perspectives on the reading will be offered. For students who have not been involved in small groups, talking and listening with a partner can be a comfortable way to learn about social interaction.

Type of Literature Experience

Shared book sets, multiple copies of particular pieces of literature, were a common choice for discussion when teachers and students first began exploring literature circles (Smith, 1990; Watson & Davis, 1988). In the shared book approach, students in a particular circle read the same book and then meet to explore in depth their different interpretations of and responses to it. Collecting multiple copies of particular books takes time, however, so some teachers began to use text sets in literature circles. Text sets include single copies of books closely related in some way— by theme, author, illustrator, genre, or cultural origin, for example (Short, 1992). Usually the set contains a range of literature that will provide readers with different perspectives on a common topic. Students in each circle read different books from the text set, meet to share their books, and search for connections among them. While shared book discussions involve an intensive look at one book, text set discussions include more retelling and focus on broad connections and comparisons across literature. With text sets, readers begin to see pieces of literature as part of a larger whole and become aware of diverse perspectives on similar topics in their search for connections among the books circle members have read.

Text set discussions can initially be overwhelming to readers, so some teachers use paired books for early literature circle discussions. With this approach, two books that present contrasting or alternative perspectives are read by all students in a circle. Paired books give students a chance to have an in-depth experience with literature while still focusing on connections and comparisons between texts (Short & Armstrong, 1993).

In some classrooms, literature-circle discussions take the form of a sharing group. In these groups, readers share books they have chosen to read independently. Because the books are unrelated, these groups rarely move beyond retelling to the more critical evaluations found in the discussions of other literature circles. These groups do help students feel more comfortable talking with one another, however, and their peers' descriptions of books they have enjoyed also encourage students to broaden their reading.

Regardless of the way the books are chosen or the circles organized, a variety of literature and other reading material can be used for discussion. Students can explore fiction, nonfiction, picture books, short stories, novels, poetry, and folklore. Stories from oral traditions can be introduced on audiotape or by storytellers. Children's own stories are often good choices for literature circle discussions. Shared book sets and text sets can include quality literature from basal readers or excerpts from content area textbooks; text sets can include magazine and newspaper articles, maps, pamphlets, and related material such as audio- and videotapes of music, storytelling, or dance, art prints, and sculpture. Text sets and shared book sets can also include books in children's first languages. When multilingual texts or translations are made available, students can read in their first language and participate in a circle that is not created solely on the basis of language.

The literature chosen for discussion is negotiated between teachers and students based on curricular goals, student interests, and availability of materials. The central criterion, however, should be that the literature chosen creates powerful story worlds with issues and connections that invite discussion for particular readers at a particular time.

Organization of the Circle Experience

Once the literature has been chosen, a student or the teacher introduces the selections through a book talk. Students then have the opportunity to browse through the books to decide which they find most appealing. We find it helpful to have more books available than there are circles, so that all the students have a choice. Some teachers post a sheet that lists the shared book and text sets and has slots for names to allow students to sign up on a first come, first served basis; other teachers determine circle membership by having students fill out a ballot with their first, second, and third choices. The exact method of forming the literature circles is less important than preserving the crucial element of student choice, for with choice comes student ownership in the process.

Once the circles are formed, students begin reading the books. In some classrooms, students who have chosen longer books read several chapters, meet to discuss those chapters, agree on how much they will read before the next meeting, and then repeat the cycle. By discussing as they read, these students can clarify confusing aspects of the story and support one another on an ongoing basis. This is especially helpful for students who are reading books not written or available in their first language.

In other classrooms, students read an entire book before discussing it in their literature circle. Usually they are given a week for a "chapter book," completing the reading during school and as homework. Students may meet daily for a few minutes to set goals for their reading and to share and clarify their initial responses, questions, and understandings with one another; the actual literature circle meeting occurs after they have had their own lived-through experience with the book and can bring a broader perspective to the discussion.

Text set circles usually move back and forth between reading and discussing. At the beginning, students often browse through the books in a set and choose one or two to read alone or with a partner. The circle then meets to share the books and to explore initial connections. In most cases, the students spend the next day or two reading other books in the set before coming back for further discussion and comparison. They often become so interested in the other books that they end up reading all or most of the books in the set.

Because students are given a choice in the literature they read and discuss and are not grouped by ability, they sometimes choose books they cannot yet read independently. We have found that those students can usually read the books with a partner or by listening and reading along with a tape. We believe that the most important aspect of literature circles is the focus on meaning-making through discussion and so are not concerned if students cannot read the books by themselves.

Kindergarten and first grade readers offer a different challenge because many are unable to read independently the kinds of books that can sustain an in-depth discussion; we have also found that young children often need to hear a story several times before they can talk about it effectively. One possibility is to read the book aloud to the circle or to have it available on tape. Usually teachers read the book aloud a number of times over several days so that students really come to know it. "Reading buddies" from older grades or parent volunteers can also read the book aloud to circle members. Other early elementary teachers send books home in special packets for three or four days so family members or friends can read them aloud. The packet usually includes a letter to the family, a piece of paper for the child to use to write or draw a response to the book, and a removable sticker the child can put on a page he or she wants to discuss with circle members.

In some classrooms, literature circles all meet at the same time; in others, one circle meets with the teacher while other students are reading independently, writing in journals, working in centers, working on other projects, or meeting on their own in their literature circles. Meetings usually begin with students sharing their impressions of and personal responses to the books. They share favorite parts, retell sections, discuss parts they found confusing, make connections to their own lives or to other literature, and engage in social chatter. This time for "mucking around" allows them to explore a wide range of ideas without focusing on one. They are not expected to write summaries, answer specific questions, or analyze literary elements, but simply to share their enjoyment of the book.

At first, students who have not experienced literature discussions may be fairly quiet or make comments that do not go beyond "I liked it" or "It was boring." It is possible that these children's past school experiences have not encouraged them to be active readers who enter into a story or discuss their understanding with other readers. These students need time, patience, encouragement, and frequent demonstrations from teacher and classmates of active and critical thinking about reading. Suggesting that children write or draw their responses in special literature logs will give them a chance to reflect on their individual experiences before meeting in their circles. In some classrooms, students make brief notes about their thinking and use them when they want to share.

Once readers have had a chance to share their initial responses, their questions, connections, and reactions will lead them to develop a more specific focus for the discussion and they will begin to move back and forth between sharing personal responses and engaging in critical dialogue. For this dialogue to be successful, readers must be willing not only to share their thinking but to listen and give consideration to the ideas of others. The discussion must also be the circle members' own; teachers can suggest possibilities for discussion if a group is having difficulty getting started, but the actual focus grows from the readers themselves. One strategy to help students move from "mucking around" to "focusing in" on an issue is to have them make a web of everything they can think of that interests them in their book or text set and then to choose an issue or question from the web for discussion. Students might also develop charts or story maps to help them sort out comparisons among books. When teachers are themselves members of a literature circle, they act as participants who share thoughts, connections, and responses to books rather than as questioners who determine the direction of discussion.

We find it helpful to have circles decide at the end of one meeting what their focus will be for the next. Students are then responsible for thinking about what they want to discuss in relation to their focus. This preparation might involve rereading sections of the book, writing, or further research.

Discussions on one book or set of books can last anywhere from two days to three weeks. Once a group has finished discussing its book or text set, the members decide whether they want to share the literature informally with the class or take time to put together a formal presentation—such as a skit or mural—about it. Children often want time to read other books related to their discussion focus or books that were read and shared by other circles; many also want time to read their own "free choice" books before starting a new round of literature circles.

Literature Circles in Action

We have found that the longer we are involved with literature circles, the more ways we find to make decisions with our students about how the discussions will be organized. These decisions add variety to classroom experiences and allow the curriculum to become more responsive to the needs of the children and the school system. To give a sense of how these decisions are considered in a particular setting with specific students, we want to share two experiences. The first comes from a collaborative project between Kathy Short and Junardi Armstrong, a second grade teacher in Tucson, Arizona; the second comes from Charlene Klassen's fourth grade classroom in Fresno, California.

Literature in Science: More Than Facts

At a school inservice program, I (Kathy) was approached by Junardi Armstrong, a second grade teacher who wanted to explore ways of bringing more literature into her classroom. Because of her background in environmental science, much of her curriculum was organized around science themes, and so it seemed logical to focus on literature as a way to learn science.

Junardi's class was beginning a unit on ecosystems that would lead to specific inquiries based on students' interests. In addition to conducting experiments, observing ecosystems in the school yard, and creating working models of ecosystems in the classroom, the children would use literature to support their science inquiries. Because we wanted students to explore the parts of an ecosystem from different perspectives, we decided to use text sets. After some initial exploration, the students joined a literature circle that would focus on plants, animals, birds, humans, insects, water, or homes and received a set of fiction and nonfiction picture books related to the topic. Students had several days to browse through their sets, and then each chose a book to read before the first literature circle meeting. Each circle kept a journal for noting anything members wanted to remember from the books.

The groups met at the same time. As Junardi and I observed and participated in them, many problems became apparent. The children enjoyed the reading, but their discussions were primarily retellings of the books, lists of isolated facts, and reports on one another's behavior. We realized that their focus on facts grew from their experiences in basal reading groups and from the class focus on scientific information. We had not provided demonstrations of alternate ways to read and talk about literature and science, so the children followed the old models.

We began reading science-related fiction and nonfiction aloud to the class and having short whole-class discussions before the children separated into their circles. We also introduced other ways of responding to stories to encourage children to enjoy the story experience and not just read literature to find facts. For example, one day each circle received a shared book set related to its focus. Students read the book alone or with a partner and then sketched the meaning of the story. They then shared their sketches in their circles as a way to begin their discussion. This involved the children in thinking about and responding more deeply to the story experience, as well as in using the story as a source of scientific information.

Junardi and I continued to struggle with how to integrate literature into science more fully. If literature is simply another vehicle for transmitting facts that could be found in encyclopedias or textbooks, then integrating literature and science adds nothing significant to children's learning. We felt that literature *could* add a rich, aesthetic perspective to the ecosystems study and wanted the children to experience the story world as well as to use literature as a source of information.

When the class moved from a focus on ecosystems in general to a study of the desert ecosystem in which the children lived, Junardi and I tried some new strategies to support students in their exploration. Students had a week to browse through various materials on the desert and then were asked to draw or write about everything they knew and felt about the desert. After the children shared their work, we brainstormed as a class. The students' responses went beyond facts, and we encouraged them to continue discussing what they were feeling *and* learning about the desert when we moved into the literature and outdoor activities that were part of the study.

Earlier we had observed that the children had difficulty making connections among the books in their first text sets. We thought this might have been due to a too-broad focus in the sets and therefore started using smaller sets with a more specific focus. For example, one week each four-member literature circle used paired books with related themes or topics, one of which was set in the desert. Two children read and discussed each of the books, and the circle then met to share the books and make comparisons.

These paired-book discussions were quite successful. The children made many connections and comparisons among the books and learned how the desert habitat was both similar to and different from other habitats in its effect on the lives of people and animals. One group, for example, read Brinton Turkle's *Thy Friend, Obadiah*, set in New England, and Byrd Baylor's *Amigo*, set in the desert. The two books tell of the friendship of a child and an animal. The group talked about the differences and similarities in the plots, animals, and climate, clothing, and housing of the story settings. Ben pointed out, "Both animals went after the boys to be their friends, but both boys had to train the animals how to act with humans. I wonder if the animals had to train the boys, too." These discussions were so productive that the children decided that each circle would put together and present to the class a chart or diagram to illustrate how their two books compared.

Webbing was an important part of the desert unit, and we demonstrated its use as part of whole-class discussions. After children shared their books in their literature circles, we asked them to make a web of everything about their books that they could discuss in more depth. Webbing became a way to organize their thinking so they could focus later discussions and use them for deeper exploration and reflection. As Ana noted, "Webbing helps me know what I really think about something. I can organize what I think."

During the several months of the ecosystem and desert studies, we moved back and forth between shared book sets, text sets, and paired books. Decisions about the most appropriate types of circles were based on the materials we had available and on whether students needed to search out connections or consider a particular issue in depth. We also felt it was important to give children a chance to read a broad range of books related to the topic. When we began the desert unit, we gathered many books on the desert and gave the children a week to browse through or read them before we began any type of literature circle. These books provided a context within which students could discuss their literature-circle books in greater depth, and they continued to explore the entire collection throughout the unit.

These many types of engagement with literature were important in broadening children's perspectives and experiences in science. The aesthetic and affective dimensions of learning were integrated into the curriculum and gave children a richer experience than when the focus was exclusively on the cognitive and factual aspects of learning. They realized that literature and science both involve living and feeling life and not just knowing about it. The children made connections among books, various aspects of nature, their life and school experiences, their own and their class-mates' ideas, different ways of knowing about science, and science and literary concepts. If we are unable to make such connections, our learning remains fragmented and we are unable to understand our world. These children's search for connections gave depth and meaning to their inquiries and allowed them to make sense of their experiences.

Peace and Conflict in a Multicultural Community

One inquiry study I (Charlene) initiated with my students was on peace and conflict. The study grew out of these fourth graders' experiences and our use of literature as a way of knowing about social, political, and cultural issues. Our classroom reflected the diversity of neighborhood cultures and included Hmong, Laotian, Cambodian, Mexican-American, African-American, and European-American students. Many students were recent immigrants to the United States and were in the class for only a short time while their families found permanent places to settle. While this cultural plurality created tension, the multiple perspectives it offered was also a potential tool for learning.

In the aftermath of a local gang incident in late December, students wanted to talk about gangs and other neighborhood problems. After several whole-class discussions in which students expressed their disbelief and fears, we decided to initiate an inquiry study. Because this study involved real social, political, and cultural problems in our neighborhood, I felt a responsibility to provide my students with an opportunity to reflect on their own histories in light of the complexities of their current experiences. Our peace and conflict study was designed to build on the past to understand the present and to envision a new future; it was also intended to facilitate a greater understanding of our neighborhood and world.

We began the study by reading and discussing picture and chapter books as a whole class to explore local and global concerns and hone the questions for our inquiry. Since half the students spoke Spanish, Hmong, Lao, or Khmer as their first language and some had only recently arrived in the United States from refugee camps, reading books in English was difficult. I chose four works for the literature circles that I thought would support students at various levels of reading proficiency and move beyond the facts of history to develop a "sense of history, a personal perspective, and a wisdom...to examine the present and project the future" (Baldwin, 1981, p. 239): Eleanor Coerr's *Sadako and the Thousand Paper Cranes*, Margaret Davidson's *I Have a Dream: The Story of Martin Luther King, Jr.*, Bette Bao Lord's *In the Year of the Boar and Jackie Robinson*, and Yoshiko Uchida's *A Jar of Dreams*. The books were introduced with book talks and the circles were formed according to students' ballots of their first and second choices.

Each group met every other day. This frequent interaction within the circles provided support for all students, whether they were reading in their first, second, or third language. If students felt they needed or wanted additional support during reading time, they chose a reading partner from their circle. When students were not reading and responding individually or with a partner or discussing the books in their circles, they were involved in literacy experiences that extended their learning. These included listening to authors on tape, recording themselves reading a favorite piece of literature, dramatizing favorite portions of a book, and reading poems, songs, picture books, and books written by classmates.

Because of the students' language backgrounds, participating in literature circles was not a simple matter. The range of English proficiency created both dilemmas and opportunities for growth. One of many issues that required constant negotiation was deciding on the number of pages to be read for subsequent group meetings. Some children could finish 20 pages a day while others struggled to read just a few. The students proposed that they negotiate a *minimum* number of pages that all group members would read before the next meeting. Individuals could read as much as they wanted, but only the pages read by all group members would be discussed in the literature circle. The 40-percent attrition rate among students led to further uncertainties about what we could expect from one another during literature circles. Talking about these problems in literature circles and negotiating and renegotiating readings for the week helped us gain a greater perspective on the diversity in reading proficiencies.

Compromise was essential in our efforts to maintain a collaborative spirit. Many students had not experienced learning as a collaborative process. I participated as a member of each literature discussion on a rotating basis in order to demonstrate collaboration and ways that one person could take up another's ideas and extend the thinking of both (Barnes, 1976/1992).

As one literature group read and discussed *A Jar of Dreams*, the tale of a Japanese girl's struggle to find acceptance in a new country, the students responded sympathetically. A Laotian boy commented that it was important to "believe in yourself and keep trying"; a Hmong girl stated, "When I was in kindergarten, I was lonely and shy." Another student extended the discussion by commenting on the conflict between ethnic groups in the book and expressing hope that Hmongs and Laotians would find peace. In the midst of reflective thought, readers felt free to pose questions about English words they did not know. Tua asked the group to clarify the word "suicide"; Beatrice felt confident enough to admit she did not know where Japan was located, which prompted us to get out maps and search. (I subsequently brought maps to all the other literature groups). Our different histories as learners provided us with a range of topics for consideration.

The book I believed to be the least powerful—*I Have a Dream: The Story of Martin Luther King, Jr.*—proved to have a profound impact on one group. Responses to it covered a range of issues. The question "What is a boycott?" led to an extensive discussion about the civil rights movement and the enslavement of various peoples throughout the world's history. Teresa connected the book's use of a derogatory term for African-Americans with terms she had heard used about Mexican-Americans, her own people. Andrea wondered if "Rosa Parks was related to Martin Luther King." Luis posed a fundamental question about cultural conflict: "I wonder why white people didn't like black people?" Jesse, who knew a great deal about gang activity from his home life, shared a comment about the kind of world in which he wanted to live: "I wish there was peace on earth." Political and historical perspectives were considered as Felicia wondered why the current president did not help the African-American people more, and Angel connected the lack of presidential intervention to the present by stating, "Our president now is closing down welfare." Chanthalansy seemed to sum up the reason for our study of peace and conflict when he explained, "Martin did get revenge. It's not revenge of killing, but revenge of peace."

Reflecting and responding through writing, drawing, or discussing with a partner before literature circles was important for all the students. They brought their literature logs to circle meetings and used them as references in discussion. Many topics were considered by the students privately before they were courageous enough to share their thoughts in the circle. Often the first entry in a literature log was a personal response to the text. When we began *I Have a Dream*, students sympathized with Martin Luther King, Jr. in writing. One African-American student, Jenifer, showed her understanding of King's experience when, as a five-year-old, his "friend" would no longer play with him because he was black:

> I had a friend like that and she was prejudice of me. I never noticed until one day, I called her and her mom answered the phone and said that she's gone and so I went over to her house and she answered the door and I said your mom said that you wasn't here and my friend said, "Oh my mom said you and me can't play together" and I just walked away and I cried. It just isn't fair.

Jenifer read her reflections to our literature circle and later to the class, and they prompted several refugee students to write about their life histories. While these students had difficulty sharing orally in English, they were willing to write down their thoughts.

Some members of the literature circle reading *In the Year of the Boar and Jackie Robinson* discussed the anger and frustration they felt about their status as refugees in a new land. I did not understand the root of their feelings, so I suggested they write about it in their literature logs. One student wrote forcefully about her perceptions of the United States' involvement in Vietnam and the resentment she felt at America's role in her homeland. She did not want to read this literature log entry aloud but agreed that I could read it to the class anonymously. Her reflections prompted a whole-class discussion about America's role in the Vietnam War. Of course, we didn't all agree, but our classroom was gradually becoming a community where students could pose difficult questions for reflection and inquiry and where all perspectives would be valued.

In addition to the literature circle meetings, our class explored concerns about peace and conflict throughout the day. In writing workshop, many students chose to write pieces about their journeys to America and the struggles they faced; in music, we sang songs such as "Let There Be Peace on Earth." During one whole-class discussion, the students voiced concerns about the personal, community, and global problems of gangs, kidnapping, robberies, murder, drugs, and alcoholism. Once we had completed the books selected for our literature circles, we formed "expert" groups based on the issues students wanted to investigate. They gathered information on their group's topic by conducting interviews and surveys, watching television, reading newspapers, magazines, and books, and reflecting on their own personal experiences. This mass of information was used to write scripts for "Kids' Court." In this culminating activity, we tried "defendants" and videotaped the trials. Parents were invited to a "peace luncheon" where we shared our video and gave speeches on our current understanding about peace and conflict.

Our classroom did not magically evolve into an environment of peaceful coexistence. Conflict still existed; in fact, sometimes it seemed more vocal than ever. What had changed was our willingness to discuss the contradictions and complexities of living in a pluralistic society. The problems we posed together were not necessarily solvable in our present context, but we were willing to begin the process by hearing voices different from our own. By negotiating our curriculum, we discovered possibilities for learning that we would never have considered individually.

Making Choices, Finding Connections

From children, we learned that literature circles offer all readers the opportunity to become active, critical thinkers. The decisions students and teachers make about the focus of literature circles, desired type of experiences, circle membership and organization, and the books chosen affect the kinds of talk and inquiry that evolve from these intensive discussions. The options Kathy, Junardi, and the second grade students chose resulted in discussion that included and then went beyond the factual aspects of ecosystems; their choices allowed them to consider aesthetic ways of knowing in scientific inquiry. Decisions made by Charlene and her fourth grade learners created a context for talk about the multiple perspectives present in the classroom and larger community. Plurality in their classroom became a productive tool for exploring social, political, and cultural complexities in the world.

Our experiences present only some of the many options available for learners as they construct new understandings through literature circles. As readers discuss literature, they come to see connections among themselves, their peers, literature, and life. They experience diverse voices that create new possibilities for growth, help shape an optimal environment for critical reflection, and play a pivotal role in transforming learning. The following voices of children demonstrate the powerful nature of the dialogue that occurs in these groups and changes the participants' understandings about learning and the world:

> In literature circles, everyone has a chance to give their opinion and even if you don't agree with that person, you keep on talking because you know that you will get more ideas. You aren't trying to figure out one right answer. In reading groups, when someone gave the right answer, we were done talking. In literature circles, we keep on going. We try to come up with as many different directions as possible.
>
> *Chris, grade three*
>
> Literature circles changed me in my eyesight, and in my brain, too.
>
> *Karen, grade three*
>
> Because I accept everyone in my class, it is easier to understand and accept people in the world for their differences.
>
> *Miranda, grade three*

References

Baldwin, R.S. (1981). When was the last time you bought a textbook just for kicks? In E. Dishner, T. Bean, & J. Readence (Eds.), *Reading in the content areas: Improving classroom instruction* (pp. 239-249). Dubuque, IA: Kendall/Hunt.

Barnes, D. (1976/1992). *From communication to curriculum.* Portsmouth, NH: Heinemann.

Calkins, L. (1990). *Living between the lines.* Portsmouth, NH: Heinemann.

Edelsky, C., Altwerger, B., & Flores, B. (1990). *Whole language: What's the difference?* Portsmouth, NH: Heinemann.

Goodman, Y.M. (1988). Exploring the power of written language through literature for children and adolescents. *The New Advocate, 1*(4), 254-265.

Hanssen, E. (1990). Planning for literature circles: Variations in focus and structure. In K.G. Short & K.M. Pierce (Eds.), *Talking about books: Creating literate communities.* Portsmouth, NH: Heinemann.

Peterson, R., & Eeds, M. (1990). *Grand conversations: Literature groups in action.* New York: Scholastic.

Rosenblatt, L.M. (1978). *The reader, the text, and the poem.* Carbondale, IL: Southern Illinois Press.

Short, K.G. (1992). Making connections across literature and life. In K. Holland, R. Hungerford, & S. Ernst (Eds.), *Journeys among children responding to literature.* Portsmouth, NH: Heinemann.

Short, K.G., & Armstrong, J. (1993). More than facts: Exploring the role of talk in classroom inquiry. In K. Pierce & C. Gilles (Eds.), *Cycles of meaning: Conversation, story, and dialogue in learning communities.* Portsmouth, NH: Heinemann.

Smith, K. (1990). Entertaining a text: A reciprocal process. In K.G. Short & K.M. Pierce (Eds.), *Talking about books: Creating literate communities.* Portsmouth, NH: Heinemann.

Watson, D., & Davis, S. (1988). Readers and texts in a fifth-grade classroom. In B. Nelms (Ed.), *Literature in the classroom.* Urbana, IL: National Council of Teachers of English.

Children's Books

Baylor, B. (1963). *Amigo.* New York: Macmillan.

Coerr, E. (1977). *Sadako and the thousand paper cranes.* New York: Dell.

Davidson, M. (1986). *I have a dream: The story of Martin Luther King, Jr.* New York: Scholastic.

Lord, B.B. (1984). *In the year of the boar and Jackie Robinson.* New York: HarperCollins.

Turkle, B. (1969). *Thy friend, Obadiah.* New York: Viking.

Uchida, Y. (1981). *A jar of dreams.* New York: Macmillan.

Citation Index

Indexes

Children's Book Author Index

Children's Book Title Index

Also available from IRA...

Bernice E. Cullinan is an acknowledged expert in the fields of literacy learning and children's literature. As a widely published author, popular convention speaker, teacher, publisher, and leader within the reading profession, she has spread the word about the importance of books and reading to a worldwide audience. In addition to *Children's Voices* IRA has available two volumes edited by Bernice Cullinan that are "must haves" for any professional collection.

- *Invitation to Read: More Children's Literature in the Reading Program* is a follow-up to the bestselling 1987 publication *Children's Literature in the Reading Program.* Included are chapters on topics such as books for emergent readers, theme units, organizing a literature-based reading program, and working with at-risk readers. A foreword by Tomie dePaola and an afterword by Bill Martin Jr frame this hands-on volume with personal accounts of the importance of books and reading. (IRA publication no. 371-622, US$18.00, US$12.00 for IRA members)

- *Fact and Fiction: Literature across the Curriculum* gives practical information for integrating literature in social studies, math, and science classes. The essays included suggest books and methods for enlivening history with historical fiction, promoting multicultural understanding with literature from and about different cultures, sparking interest in social studies with informational titles, teaching math concepts with favorite children's stories, and supplementing science textbooks with trade books on science-related topics. *Fact and Fiction* shows you how to let literature be the thread that runs through teaching and learning across the elementary grades. (IRA publication no. 380-622, US$15.00, US$10.00 for IRA members)

For information about IRA publications or to place your order, call 1-800-336-READ, ext. 266 (outside the United States or Canada, call 302-731-1600, ext. 266). Visa and MasterCard accepted; postage included on prepaid orders.